The Philosophical Dimension of Psychology
A Beginner's Guide

James A. Harold

Pepperdine University,
Franciscan University of Steubenville

Cognitive Science and Psychology

VERNON PRESS

www.vernonpress.com

In the Americas:
Vernon Press
1000 N West Street, Suite 1200
Wilmington, Delaware, 19801
United States

In the rest of the world:
Vernon Press
C/Sancti Espiritu 17,
Malaga, 29006
Spain

Cognitive Science and Psychology

Library of Congress Control Number: 2021942327

ISBN: 978-1-64889-363-6

Also available: 978-1-62273-963-9 [Hardback]; 978-1-64889-333-9 [PDF, E-Book]

Cover Design: By Edith Harold
Front cover: "Psyche in relation to a Transcendent World of Beauty, Goodness and Truth"
Back Cover: "Freud's Psyche: Cold, Unmoored, Aimless"

Dedicated to

Ronda Chervin

My First Philosophy Professor

Thank You

Table of Contents

Acknowledgments

There has to be a special place in heaven for readers of philosophy texts in progress. Thank you, Teresa Harold, my dear wife, for your copy editing. Thank you, Philip Harold, Paul Vitz, Matthew Breuninger, C. M. Wulf and James Beauregard, for your wonderful suggestions and help. Thank you, Professor James Beauregard, for putting me in contact with Vernon Press. Thank you, Vernon Press, for your kindness and patience. Finally, thank you, Bradford Fellmeth, for your generous, kind help with all my computer questions. There never was detected a single raised eyebrow over helping me with the very same, exact problem I experienced merely hours before. Thank you.

Foreword
by
James Beauregard

PHD
Rivier University
Clinical Neuropsychologist
Associated Scholar, Hildebrand Project

In psychoanalytic theory, when early adolescents decathect—that is, break away from their childhood relationship with their parents—they don't quite take all of their self along. There's a gap, and that gap is filled in by one's peer group. Something not dissimilar happened to psychology in the late 1800s, when it consciously broke away from its historical relationship with natural philosophy to embrace the empirical methods of the hard sciences. This process has resulted in remarkable advancements in psychology across the twentieth and now the twenty-first century. But psychology also left something behind: the wider, and balancing, world view of philosophy. Unwittingly, it embraced not only a methodology—the scientific method—, but also a world view—empiricism. This choice has not been without consequences for all of the human sciences. One of the most troubling consequences of this separation has been reductionism—the reducing of persons to the physical and the biological, and the consequent attempt to understand persons from these perspectives alone. Furthermore, many have embraced not just the reliable tenets of the empirical method, but a set of beliefs about science collectively referred to as scientism–believing that the empirical method is the only valid way of generating new knowledge, and in more extreme cases, the only valid way of knowing anything at all. This view has effectively created a type of blindness in many modern academic disciplines, specifically a failure to attend to anything about persons that is not amenable to the measurements and observations of science. As a result, some of the most important aspects of being persons fall by the wayside—love, happiness, intuition, human freedom. Harold rightly notes that the content of standard introductory textbooks in psychology presents one way of looking at the field—the empirical one. The reality of these texts is that one of the most important aspects of psychology – psychotherapy –is typically relegated to the end of the book and given only superficial attention. And yet, the vast majority of people who come into contact with a psychologist over the course of their life will do so in the context of psychotherapy. The author's phenomenological approach allows him to recognize the whole person, not only that which is amenable to objective measurement, and to help us see psychology as a complex whole. One of the chief strengths—and pleasures—of Harold's writing (to highlight one of many) is his striking ability to present philosophical concepts in a comprehensible fashion to the reader. In doing so, he has provided us with an antidote to this problem of reduction. With backgrounds in both psychology and philosophy, he is ideally positioned to recognize what psychology has lost—creating its contemporary blind spots—and to provide concrete ways of moving toward a fuller vision of persons.

This is a book that I look forward to assigning to my own psychology students to give them a vision of the discipline of psychology that is more holistic, and because of that, more adequate and more accurate about human beings. As his writing ranges across the whole field of psychology, he proves himself again and again to be a reliable guide.

Introduction

The purpose of this book is to provide the kind of text I wish would have been available to me many years ago as an undergraduate/graduate psychology student. During those times, I remember feeling a certain inadequacy and incompleteness with respect to the dominant direction of my psychology studies, such as is found in introductory psychology textbooks. I wondered if this was more a problem with me than with the content of these studies. Nobody else, whether professors or students, seemed much concerned. And besides, as a teenager, what did I know? Still, I never could quite convince myself that my feelings and concerns were baseless. I felt in some vague way that mainline psychology, despite its gold-plated scientific pedigree, seemed far too open to merely superficial cultural influences, while deeper truths about human nature were often ignored or explained away. This difficulty was not about questioning the veracity of specific scientific, psychological investigations as much as a nagging sense of incompleteness with respect to their vision concerning human nature. For example, mainline psychology seemed good at identifying irrationality but was practically silent on our rational, personal nature, while oddly presupposing such a nature as a condition for applying their scientific approach. Where were the chapters in introductory textbooks devoted to the rational powers of the intellect and will?

Still, I always thought if I could just find the right mentor, things would be far better. Of course, such mentors in psychology existed, then as well as now. Just because mainline psychology—the psychology one finds in basic textbooks—is one way does not mean all of psychology goes that way. Individual psychology mentors could easily make up for whatever deficiencies existed in mainline psychology. It was just at that particular time and place I did not find one in my psychological studies. So this feeling of the incompleteness of psychology was not corrected, at least by my teachers. It rather grew over the course of my psychology studies. It was ultimately what provoked me to abruptly change course and switch to philosophy.

I am not claiming that philosophy as a field of study is somehow in a better, saner position than psychology. Taken as a whole, it is at least as confused and confusing as psychology. It is just that in philosophy, I actually found not one or two, but rather a whole particular school of mentors. What they taught made perfect sense to me, so I had the possibility of making that vision my own. I grant that in philosophy (similar to mathematics), one needs to see with one's own eyes and not merely through the eyes of others. But practically everyone needs help from teachers, including me. I liked how my philosophy professors respected what is true and yet were willing to learn from people of every intellectual camp, including their own intellectual opponents. I am deeply indebted to them.

What I ended up doing was switching gears and getting a doctorate in philosophy. However, during those studies—and afterwards too—I was surprised to find out just how my psychological education was not terminated, but rather continued and even flourished. It gave me the novel idea, at least to myself, that philosophy had much to offer psychology. This novelty of approach surprised me because I assumed the only methodology acceptable to psychology was just what I learned in my basic introductory psychology classes (and then presupposed in all my other classes): the empirical, scientific method. But if that were true, how come I kept meeting with interesting psychological insights from philosophers who did not use that method? Then I wondered why these insights were under-represented and even neglected by mainline psychology and what this philosophical/psychological approach is?[1] Also, why not integrate that method—whatever it is—into psychology as a whole, especially if these insights could help correct some of the deficiencies of the scientific, psychological method? Similarly, the empirical psychological method could help with what is lacking with the philosophical/psychological approach. My suspicion was that the criterion (or measure) for what was considered a suitable object for psychological investigation had to first pass an empirical litmus test, which then excluded the philosophical/psychological viewpoint.

What I want to do with this book is investigate what psychology looks like without that litmus test. In my view, there will also be an opening for a philosophical contribution to psychology. This dimension can add a three-dimensional fullness to psychology that is far more satisfying and interesting than merely empirical psychology alone.

Philosophy, however, is like psychology in being extremely varied. Not every philosophy is in a position to be of real service to psychology. There are, after all, just as many crazy philosophical systems as there are psychologies. In fact, many of the wild psychologies stem from philosophy. This is no doubt one reason why many reasonable psychologists are legitimately fearful of philosophy.

Let me state first in broad terms the kind of philosophy I have in mind, which, if true, can be of service to psychology. It is a philosophy of realism, that is, a philosophy which claims that the human person can really know some aspects of reality as it is in itself. This kind of philosophy refers to the classical, philosophical tradition going back to Plato, Aristotle, Augustine and Aquinas. These people especially gave me insight into what an ordered, psychological life of a person theoretically looks like, which then allowed me to see more easily what is psychologically disordered.

Specifically, however, the philosophical approach I will be using will be the language and approach of a school known as phenomenological realism, growing out of the work of twentieth-century philosophers Edmund Husserl, Max Scheler, and Dietrich von Hildebrand. Although I will be largely using their terminology, it is important to note their connection to the great philosophical tradition of classical philosophy, that is, of philosophical realism. Many of their insights could just as easily have been transmitted using a stricter Aristotelian or Thomistic approach and categories.

I think this phenomenological approach, however, is especially suited to the project of this book. There are two advantages of phenomenology over these other classical philosophies worth mentioning.

First, phenomenological realism attempts to be especially close to a direct, intuitive, and concrete lived experience, with less reliance on learning a wholly abstract, deductive system that typically characterizes Aristotelian and Thomistic philosophizing. Psychologists in general prefer the concrete and the experiential to the abstract. However, just because the richness of the Thomistic system is largely foreign to a modern audience does not mean it is thereby false, but it does pose difficulties in applying it for my purposes.

Secondly, a realist, phenomenological approach will take into account not only objective truth—so thematic to classical philosophy—but also the subjective, conscious experience of the person encountering that truth. Realist phenomenology is interested in exploring this subjectivity, just as it is open to the possibility of the subject reaching objective reality (and responding adequately to it), as well as investigating the reasons why we sometimes fall short of being in a right relation to reality.

In one specific respect I hope to "turn the tables" on psychology, insofar as introductory psychology textbooks tend to be antiseptic (insofar as these texts require nothing from a person challenging the way they existentially live their life), third-person, and *objective*. Of course, persons are objective realities, and also beings who can be sensibly or empirically observed, so there is obviously much to be said for this approach.

There is, however, something else. There is also an existential, *subjective* dimension to our being as well. We are not just objects but also subjects, with our own interior, conscious life. That interiority refers to our own conscious, inner experience of freedom and our ability to know reality as it is in itself. Naturally, whether or not an object of study possesses an inner psychological life does not particularly impact biology, chemistry or physics. And outside of diagnosis and pain management, it hardly impacts medicine. But this inner life does impact psychology. One argument of this book is that something central to psychology is lost if this realm is ignored, discounted or at times even denied.

Mainline psychology and introductory psychology texts investigate human beings almost exclusively in that objective sense: as *objects* of psychological investigation, similar to the mode of investigation of all the other natural sciences. It is perfectly legitimate and appropriate for these sciences, including psychology, to look at persons from that point of view, especially when one understands that the term *object* is rightly understood in this context to only refer to "a datum given," without any implication of depersonalization. It is not that this approach is illegitimate; it is just not the only point of view for psychological research. It is unnecessary to argue for either a purely objective or subjective approach. There will be positives and negatives with both kinds of approaches, with neither method simply being able to replace the other without loss.

There is, however, something ironic about psychology—of all disciplines—ignoring a direct investigation of inner conscious life, insofar as one would think that one primary object of psychological investigation would be conscious life. And by *psychology*, I am again thinking of it only in its mainline sense, as represented by the *American Psychological Association* website and introductory psychology textbooks. I am sure there are individual psychologists who will share many of my criticisms of mainline psychology and feel perfectly free to focus explicitly on inner, subjective life. Furthermore, there are individual psychologists and programs, such as that at Duquesne University, who will use a phenomenological approach.

Also, I think the psychological academic landscape in general is better today than 30 years ago. Martin Seligman's positive psychology has become a major player influencing all of psychology for the better, insofar as he weakened a deterministic orientation dominating large dimensions (specifically, behavioristic psychology and psychoanalytic thought) of this field. He has refocused psychology away from an exclusive orientation towards efficient causality and towards an appreciation of the role that final causality[2] plays. To understand that things have purposes and ends presupposes the further idea that they have specific natures oriented to specific things that fulfill them. The idea that things have natures that should be respected leads back to philosophy, which is the discipline that studies the general natures (or essences) of things.

Despite the undeniable impact of positive psychology on contemporary psychology, it still remains but one voice among others. Its leaven has not yet sufficiently transformed the dough of what introductory psychology students learn in their classes. There remains a need for students to look at their field from both an empirical *and* philosophical perspective, which I hope will lead to a richer, more existential (in the sense of being more relevant to their own life) and commonsensical understanding of psychology.

Although I will be critical of contemporary psychology, I do not intend to produce here any kind of "hit-piece" against psychology. I see the value and significance of psychology, including empirical psychology. In fact, I want to broaden out its reach by bringing in philosophical, literary and even theological perspectives that I think have been neglected by mainline psychology.

Although my main focus is on psychology, I will use a philosophical approach,[3] which not only has its own method for reaching truth, but also its own content as well. And this content will at times overlap with the subject matter of psychology. The method used by philosophy is exactly the same as the one followed by mathematics and classical geometry, which allows the mind to intellectually *see* some universal truths, such as the principles of contradiction, identity, number relations, and many others besides, including insights into the nature of the human person. As this kind of *seeing* is intellectual, it is not sensual or empirical in nature. The object of philosophy extends beyond the perceiving of sensible particulars to understanding the general natures of things, including human nature: not just the nature of the person as factually given, but also the way a person ought to be.

To say that the philosophical method can be of assistance to psychology does not imply that this method can alone solve all psychological issues. Psychology may not be exclusively an empirical or natural science, but it is an empirical science. In this text, I want to be open to those psychological objects amenable to the empirical method—of sense observation and inductive generalization— as well as to those receptive to a more philosophical approach. For example, while the empirical sciences study only neutral facts, or what *is* the case, philosophy also studies (besides neutral facts) what *ought* to be. Thus, while the moral sphere is closed to a purely empirical investigation, it is open to philosophical penetration. Ethics, of course, is not psychology, but that does not mean there is no overlap between these fields. For example, without an ethical worldview one cannot do full justice either to human motivation (insofar as some persons really are motivated by what is authentically good and true) or to clearly understand what it is that constitutes self-fulfillment.

Morality, however, is just one instance of a broader pattern of measuring psychic acts and responses according to rational measures, such as when we note that a person's psychological response is either ordered or disordered, balanced or imbalanced, or one could say, rational or irrational. I want to investigate other rational, psychological measures besides morality—such as truth, health and our particular human nature—which I think can be extremely helpful for evaluating psychic responses. This is the central idea behind rational psychology, which is what psychology used to be called before its superseded by empirical psychology at the end of the nineteenth century.

If the above is in the main correct, then psychology needs to accept the notion that human persons are not simply higher-order animals, but rational beings ordered to what is true and authentically good, insofar as it is these things that are the ultimate rational measures of the person. This power of rationality, however, does not exclude the real possibility of irrational thinking and behavior, as the former is the condition for the possibility of and the measure for the latter.

This rational philosophical approach to psychology has never been completely extinguished in contemporary psychology. However, it needs to thematically re-assert its proper and far larger place within psychology, which implies as well doing justice to a philosophical approach to reality and giving up the notion that psychology is exclusively empirical in nature. This is what I want to establish in this book.

Chapter 1

Psychology, Philosophy and Common Sense

The purpose of this book is to provide a beginning reflection on the philosophical dimension to the discipline of psychology, oriented to introducing certain philosophical ideas that are central to psychology. This text is written especially with undergraduate and graduate psychology students in mind. While certain philosophical ideas will inevitably have to be introduced and explained, the "center of gravity," so to speak, will be on psychology. Since this book is ordered especially to non-philosophers, every effort will be made to be clear.*

*THE GOAL OF PHILOSOPHICAL CLARITY

Every writer should strive to be clear. Towards that end—together with the idea that readers will be primarily non-philosophers—I want to give more than the usual number of brief explanations in footnotes (any drawn-out comments in footnotes should be considered secondary, or at least more technical points), and then more extensive and central explanations of ideas and terms in "boxes," one of which you are reading now.

In the text itself the expressions—*in other words* and *that is*—will be used to say the same thing in different ways. The goal is clarity (while not being tedious). While abstract, philosophical principles will inevitably need to be stated, they also need to be explained, justified and illustrated with concrete examples. Certainly, thinking philosophically is different, so it is important to get the language straight. Alternative ways of putting things can help.

One caveat is worth emphasizing: I do not want to purchase "clarity" by simply stating conclusions without explanation and justification. The goal is to give evidence for positions, so students can see the truth of positions *for themselves*. Merely stating positions, even on the assumption of their truth, is not enough. They also need to be made evident as true, otherwise I would be merely substituting ideology (or propaganda) for philosophy. The need is for clarity *and* evidence, which will require the work of sifting and evaluating. Streamlining that away is a mistake. It is disrespectful to readers.

A central theme of this book will be a reflection on what it is that constitutes evidence for psychological, philosophical and scientific positions.

Sometimes it is good for an academic to stop, take a step back, and take a fresh look at one's own discipline. This is a task for every science, whether it be mathematics, physics, psychology or philosophy. What is the kind of reality and nature of the objects investigated by each of these sciences? In other words, what are their metaphysical* foundations? In their own nature and on their own terms: what really is number? What is matter? What does it mean to be a person? What are conscious life and psychic acts? What are the objects and methods that psychology studies? Is there some divergence between what people say they are and what they really are? Of course the objects and methods claimed by professional psychologists and contemporary psychology will be appropriate for many aspects of psychology. Are they appropriate for them all? If so, then this appropriateness should be explained and defended.

*METAPHYSICS

Metaphysics refers to the philosophy of being. The notion of *being* refers to the kind of existence things have in themselves. For example, what is it that specifies the kind of being of a person? What is it that characterizes a purely material being? What kind of being do values and words possess, as well as ideal essence structures, such as justice and truth? Are these essence structures pre-given or made-up by someone, such as by society or God? Can we make true or false assertions about them, or are they nothing but what we say they are (the thesis of idealism)? Metaphysics even studies the kind of being mere appearances and illusions possess, which also have a certain kind of psychological reality (Chapter 5).

Modern science and contemporary culture tend to think of "metaphysics" as quaint medievalism or even as slightly disreputable, as evidenced by the fact that in modern bookstores the Metaphysics section is right next to the Astrology and Palm Readings sections. But there is no escaping it. Everyone inevitably thinks metaphysically, including those scientists who otherwise think metaphysics is bunk, such as when they then think that human beings are nothing but higher-order animals. That assumption may or may not be true; either way, statements like that are metaphysical in nature.

My goal is to make explicit some of the "philosophical underpinnings" of mainline "classical" authors, such as B. F. Skinner, Sigmund Freud, and Carl Rogers, against the background of the explicitly stated positions of the *American Psychological Association* and mainline introductory psychology texts, and to do this in a straightforward, common-sense style and approach.

These philosophical underpinnings will be of two kinds: the first are very broad (formal or structural) philosophical principles which not only apply to psychology, but to every other science as well, including all the empirical sciences. For example, everyone has a sense of the principle of non-contradiction (*contradictory opposite statements cannot both be true*). While such principles are obviously important for the sciences, the primary emphasis of this text will be on those philosophical objects and principles that are more specific to psychology, such as the phenomenon of freedom, the power of the person to know truth, the non-empirical nature of psychic acts (loving, willing, despairing, etc.), the realm of value and morality, and the conscious personal self. These topics are not the usual subject matter for psychology texts. Is that because they are not psychological in nature? What are properly psychological phenomena? To answer these questions, there needs to be an investigation of what it is that psychology studies (Chapters 4 and 5). Just what is the subject matter of psychology? In this text, I will attempt to answer these questions, but only in a formal or general way, leaving out crucially important material that is the proper domain specifically of the science—as opposed to the philosophy—of psychology.*

*THE MEANING OF THE TERM *PSYCHOLOGY* IN THIS TEXT

This box will discuss the meaning of the term *psychology*. I am not yet investigating the subject matter of psychology, which is a later topic, but rather what the word, *psychology*, means in this text. This term has a specified meaning, both broader in one direction and narrower in another than the common meaning of the term.

It is broader than *empirical psychology* (knowledge based on sense perception). Naturally, everyone, including me, grants the overlap between psychology and empirical psychology. Empirical psychology is obviously part of psychology. But the work of this text will be to show that there is no simple, straightforward co-extensive identity between them as if the limits of psychology begin and end with empirical psychology.

In another direction, however, the term (*psychology*) will be here used in a narrower sense, as when *psychology* sometimes designates practically anything under the sun (similar to the term *philosophy*). This idea is too large—at least for my purposes—because it would then, on many points, be contradictory (again similar to *philosophy*), as rival psychological schools and theorists contradict each other all the time. Thus, I will mean with this term something more specific and (relatively) consistent: its mainline sense, as understood by contemporary introductory psychology textbooks and by the home webpage of the *American Psychological Association*. There is, especially given the Wild West atmosphere of psychology in general, a surprising consistency with respect to contemporary, mainline psychology textbooks.

Because I will be dealing with mainline psychology, I will to some extent be leaving out many trends in psychology that are encouraging and congenial to my own approach, such as Victor Frankl's logotherapy, Martin Seligman's positive psychology, Paul Vitz's meta-model approach of the person and Stephen Madigan's narrative or storytelling method. Although I will at times reference these approaches, I will, in the main, be looking at psychology more narrowly, from the point of view of introductory psychology texts. Although psychology is broader than this understanding, I think it remains true that most or even practically all psychology programs, graduate and undergraduate, are oriented around this mainline approach.

This investigation will critically investigate psychological themes and authors from a philosophical perspective. And by "critical" I mean not some stubborn, obnoxious or skeptical approach, but rather an attitude whereby positions are weighed by the kind and degree of the evidence presented, together with an openness to accepting what is true. It may be that a few positions contemporary psychologists and psychological texts make are unable to be empirically supported and, in fact, can really only be justified, if at all, by a philosophical approach. Thus, a critical approach can expose assertions that at times are presented as having the authority of "science," but which are actually philosophical in nature.

In this book, a sustained argument will be made that the subject matter of psychology is actually far broader than what is typically held today, and to note some reasons for this limitation. Specifically, it may be that mainline psychology is limited by its own stated empirical methodology* and its pragmatic (utilitarian) approach.** The aim of this text is to show that there is a greater context for psychological truth, one that includes more than just the empirical method and approach.

*DEFINING TERMS: *METHODOLOGY, EMPIRICAL, EMPIRICAL SCIENCE, EMPIRICAL METHOD, EMPIRICISM* AND *RATIONALISM*

A *methodology* refers simply to the way people do things. For example, some things I must observe with my senses. Other things I do not (directly) perceive or observe, but perhaps can infer (or conclude to) from other things. For example, I may infer—rightly or wrongly—that a person is a student by the university logo on her shirt. The term *empirical* refers to that which can be known through the senses or inferred from them. The main empirical or natural sciences are biology, chemistry and physics. All these sciences go back to and presuppose actual observation of really existing, sensible phenomena. Scientists learn that phenomena behave in ways that are relatively uniform and therefore generalizable and predictable. Empirical sciences involve precise measurement, but the formulation of empirical laws involves individual variations, including exceptions.

In contrast, philosophy, classical geometry and mathematics do not go back to and are not grounded in sense perception (empirical observation), insofar as these kinds of insights measure sense perception. The ultimate source of their knowledge goes back to a kind of pure understanding or intellectual intuition, such as when a person (intellectually) "sees" that 2+2=4 and that *killing innocent people for racist reasons is wrong*. These kinds of laws are invariable, as there is in principle no instance where *2+2 equals 5,*

The claim that *all* knowledge goes back only to empirical observation is called empiric*ism,* just as the claim that *all* knowledge goes back to pure philosophical/mathematical understanding is called rational*ism.* Empirical science is not identical to empiricism nor rational knowledge with rationalism. Similarly, not all metaphysical and ethical knowledge can be explained in terms of merely psychological categories, which would be psycholog*ism.* One can be fully appreciative of all these disciplines without pretending that any one of them can answer all questions.

A total empiricism and a total rationalism exclude each other, and so cannot both be true. In contrast, one does not need to choose between a limited empirical or limited rational knowledge, as both could be true in their respective and appropriate realms. For example, there is no need to apply the empirical method to establish that *2+2=4*; one can just (intellectually and rationally) see it. Such formulations then measure empirical realities, not vice versa. And from thinking alone, no one could ever establish the average boiling point of water at sea level. It has to be empirically measured.

In this text, an argument will be made that neither a pure empiric*ism* nor a pure rational*ism* alone adequately explains human knowledge. Rather, both empirical and rational knowledge exist in their own proper spheres. Each type of knowledge has its place and limits.

This book will provide some explanation and justification for a limited rational knowledge position, crucial to justifying philosophical, mathematical and geometrical knowledge, and against both rationalism and empiricism. It is, however, outside the parameters of this text to explicitly focus on it, as the primary orientation will be on psychology.

**PRAGMATISM, IDEALISM AND PSYCHOLOGY

The father of the American pragmatic movement in philosophy is also one of the founding fathers of modern psychology, William James (1842-1910). James was trained as a philosopher. He said that the first psychology lecture he ever attended was the one he himself gave, and he was deeply influenced by the thought of Immanuel Kant (1724-1804). The philosopher Kant held that we cannot know things as they are in themselves because the mind helps form the actual content of our conceptions of things. Since this forming by the intellect is done automatically—simply by the particular structure of the mind we, in fact, have as human beings—there can be no separating out what is given from the naked empirical intuition (or sense perception) from what is automatically superimposed by the mind. This means that for both James and Kant, we cannot know reality as it is in itself. So, instead of realism (the mind being formed by reality), Kant turned things around and espoused an idealism (reality that is partially formed and constituted by the mind). For Kant, what we "get" from reality— empirical sensation alone—is far too impoverished and chaotic to be knowable.[4] Thus, there is the need for "help" by the mind, not just to know, but also to provide a crucial dimension of organizing and contributing to the object known. The effect of this "organizing and contributing to the object known" is that we can never know reality simply speaking, as it is in itself. Thus, idealism ultimately leads to skepticism.

James followed in this idealist tradition, but with this twist: instead of maintaining that what is received from reality is too impoverished for knowledge, he held that what is received is too rich. One, after all, can be blinded from two directions: from too little or from too much light. Therefore, we need a principle for ordering and delimiting the welter incoming phenomena. His principle is that what is true is *what works* for the better satisfaction of a person's needs.[5] If need satisfaction is the crucial factor determining truth, then the power that effects this satisfaction becomes crucial. Thus with James, need satisfaction and power relations constitute (and thereby replace) truth.

In this text, the possibility of there being a place for both realism (knowing things as they are in themselves) and a limited pragmatic approach (looking at reality from the point of view of our needs) will be investigated. Perhaps reality can be viewed from both points of view. Maybe we really do know some things as they are in themselves, even if this knowledge will at times go against our own needs. And with the phenomena of appearances and illusions (Chapter 2), maybe there is also a subjective contribution to aspects of our subjective, conscious experience. As long as one does not presuppose that *all* experience is merely reducible to appearances and illusions, which is the thesis of idealism, both phenomena (of appearances and illusions) can exist within a general framework of realism.

Furthermore, taking an interest in truth—in knowing things simply as they are in themselves—need not negate interest in pragmatic concerns. There is, after all, a legitimate practical, therapeutic dimension to psychology.

To my mind, one of the most important philosophical issues surrounding modern psychology (which needs to be established in this text as it is not immediately evident) concerns the tension between realism (that we can know reality as it is in itself) and idealism/pragmatism.* This tension can be explained as arising out of empiricism. Insofar as practically all of modern psychology claims that facts are inherently empirical, it follows that all theory not closely tied to empirical facts becomes thereby merely speculative in nature, a superimposition of mind onto this factual, empirical knowledge.[6] Since speculation inevitably goes beyond empirical facts, idealism arises when people think they are free to "superimpose their own ideas," or alternatively, to construct theories along the lines of "what works" (pragmatism) to fulfill needs. The question is whether psychology extends beyond the acknowledgment of empirical facts to embrace "purely rational or philosophical facts" as well. If so, we can then have another source of knowledge and truth going beyond pragmatic/idealist interpretations. Realism will then be more strongly affirmed.

*IS THE DEBATE BETWEEN REALISM AND IDEALISM REALLY SIGNIFICANT FOR PSYCHOLOGY?

The debate between realism and idealism is primarily philosophical in nature. However, an idealist frame of reference has slipped into not only psychology but also our culture as a whole, at least in these three ways:

First, there is the strong impetus in the culture—driven by philosophers like Jean Paul Sartre—to think that there are no inherent meanings in things, and therefore all meaning merely comes from what we superimpose upon reality.

Second, this superimposition then leads to what Robert Barron terms an "ideology of self-invention,"[7] as if what we are is simply reducible to what we think or merely desire ourselves to be.

Finally (third), this orientation towards idealism will affect not only our own overall psychological self-definition, it will also affect our approach to a whole spectrum of particular psychological issues, from anorexia nervosa, body dysmorphic disorder (BDD), body integrity identity disorder (BIID) to transgenderism, discussed later (Chapter 8). Thus, someone with an idealist frame of reference will emphasize getting reality to conform to their own way of thinking, while a realist will emphasize getting the person to conform to reality.

Psychology needs to be aware of these basic philosophical/cultural influences, even if they are otherwise merely implicit, as they can influence very concrete therapeutic counseling issues, seemingly far removed from philosophy. It is naïve to think that psychology is simply motivated by empirical facts alone.

I want to show that the methodological decision to declare the subject matter of *all* psychology to be empirical in nature (empiric*ism* or scient*ism**) is not reducible merely to an ivory tower squabble about method. These methodological presuppositions will have a tremendous impact on what is then considered a proper object or subject matter of psychological investigation. An exclusively empirical or pragmatic approach can become a prism through which psychology—and everything else—is seen. Certain things will be recognized while other things will hardly be seen at all, despite their real psychological significance. One example to illustrate this point: empirical psychology is far more comfortable talking about causal relations than freedom, which in introductory psychology textbooks is hardly discussed.[8] Why? One reason may be because causal relations can be found in material things that can (generally speaking[9]) be sensibly observed. But freedom—if it exists—is not an empirical datum, as it is not empirically given. Furthermore, from a purely pragmatic perspective which only measures "what works," whether a psychic act is free or determined will be irrelevant, if the effects are the same.

*SCIENTISM

Closely associated with empiricism is scientism, which is the view that *all* knowledge is ultimately scientific in nature. If all real facts are empirical facts, then it follows that the hard sciences (biology, chemistry, physics, etc.) will ultimately have the last word adjudicating all issues. Since philosophy is not a hard science using the empirical method of observation and induction, the investigation of the "content" or "subject matter" for knowledge has to be found elsewhere. This relegates philosophy to the role of merely assessing the language used by scientists, such as making sure the logic follows and the terms are consistent and unambiguous, which is exactly the view of a particular branch of philosophy called logical positivism. In this approach, there is no distinct content that philosophy investigates.

This general idea is deeply ingrained within our culture. The new gurus of today are the scientists, or at least the scientific popularizers. Look for their spokesmen and women on TV. Sometimes they will even dress the part, taking on priest-like garb. And since the hard sciences are where the real action is, it then makes sense that contemporary psychology similarly wants to see itself as belonging in that camp.

An exclusively empiricistic and pragmatic/utilitarian emphasis within modern psychology not only limits but also slants our psychological understanding of the person towards instincts, needs, and neuroses, insofar as they are more easily studied scientifically. The notions of freedom, truth, knowledge, beauty, goodness, love, and what genuinely fulfills a person will be discounted because they go in a more philosophical direction. This slant is reductionistic, insofar as they explain higher realities in terms of lower ones (such as with the above example of freedom being explained by mere causality), thereby ignoring or explaining away the higher dimension of human nature. I think there is no need to overemphasize or ignore one aspect or the other, as both dimensions can be found within human nature.

While this text will focus primarily on psychology, albeit from a philosophical point of view, it is worth mentioning other contexts for psychological truth. They are to be found also in literature and even in theology,[10] as well as in other psychological dimensions found only in our (non-theoretical, non-empirically accessible) naïve lived experience.*[11] All these various contexts of psychology— not just the empirical side—are important for getting at a proper understanding of psychological realities. This is the central theme of this book: psychology is not exclusively empirical, and psychologists need to be open to other avenues of investigation.

*LIVED EXPERIENCE

I will periodically reference the idea of *lived experience*. It refers to a direct, naive contact with reality. It is naive—not here implying anything pejorative—but rather indicating its direct, unreflective and non-theoretical character. This kind of contact can be real—such as with an experience of really existing things—or it can be illusory, as when a person's experience does not correspond to the way things really are. Either way, there is a direct givenness of the phenomenon experienced, as opposed to when a person "takes a step back," so to speak, and reflects back upon that experience. The advantage of "thinking about things" in a more reflective way is that one has a chance to better distinguish between whether some experience is real or illusory. The advantage of lived experience is its closeness to reality. Reflection without being grounded and guided by lived experience leads to "ivory tower" thinking.

There is a philosophical system that is especially devoted to being faithful to "naïve lived experience," called phenomenology. This philosophy goes back to an early twentieth-century philosopher, Edmund Husserl (1859-1938), whose famous battle-cry was "back to the things themselves,"[12] with the "things" being those realities given to us in our lived experience. He wanted us to get away from an overly theoretical, abstract thinking and return to our lived experience. He thereby exposed the real danger of merely projecting our own ideas onto experience. This point is important for everyone doing philosophy as it is, oddly enough, often easier to merely superimpose our theories onto reality than to actually look to find out what really is the case.

One important theme of this text will be to show the philosophical dimension of the science of psychology. These philosophical influences can be explicit and frankly admitted, or they can be denied and thereby remain unexamined. This is not from any nefarious plot. It is just one unintended consequence of psychology's love affair with empirical science and method, as if *all* the data needed for psychological research is an application of the experimental method.[13] Naturally, if this last point is true, then philosophy really is irrelevant to psychology.

The idea here is not to create a "two-track" psychological system—one going back to empirical science and the other philosophy—but rather to integrate the empirical and philosophical dimensions together into a single vision of psychological reality having at least two dimensions, with each dimension helping to interpret and explain the other.

Consider again, for example, freedom: one can interpret empirical facts either with or without this supposition. Whether or not a particular act is free goes back to other aspects of our lived experience of reality rather than to any empirical fact. There are times in which we simply do not know, exclusively on the basis of the behavior of others, how freely they intended some action in a particular situation. I could easily think, for instance, that you intended to trip me—*you did this on purpose!*—when in fact the action was a sheer accident, or vice versa. And yet, even if the effect is exactly the same—I got tripped!—we all know it makes a tremendous difference whether that trip was intentional (thus going back to freedom) or not.

There is a tendency in contemporary psychology to look at its own field in an insulated way, that is, as a scientific discipline that is largely independent of wider contexts. Such an approach tends to characterize not only contemporary psychology, but all the natural sciences (biology, physics, and chemistry) as well. For instance, while courses in the humanities might benefit chemists *as persons*, it is much harder to see how they help them do chemistry, as a more insulated analytical* approach (rightly) dominates this field.

*CONTRASTING ANALYTIC AND SYNTHETIC APPROACHES TO UNDERSTANDING

An analytic approach is one in which someone can view an object of study by dividing it up into its parts, thereby trying to understand the whole in terms of its parts. This point of view appropriately dominates the empirical, natural sciences. In contrast, a synthetic approach goes in the opposite direction, that is, of making connections from one thing to another such that, in the end, a person has a sense for the whole.

A concrete example will help explain the significance of these terms. I knew a man who once ran a medium-sized rubber manufacturing company making rubber products for bathrooms. He told me that he employed two chemists on his staff who were smart guys, smarter than he was and very good at the applied chemistry needed for his business. He also thought that despite their high intelligence, they would be disastrous at running his company because they only thought only in terms of applied chemistry. Whereas, in contrast, as president, he had to think not only analytically or in parts but also in terms of the good of the whole, that is, of the point of view of his whole business. Purely analytical thinking could be disastrous for large entities, such as a university or a state, as it can lead to overemphasizing one facet at the expense of others. Synthetical thinking is especially important for being a philosopher as philosophy strives to achieve a sense for the whole of reality.

The problem, of course, is that this synthetic sensibility is not the only talent needed for running things. One also needs to possess administrative skills going in a more analytic direction. We all know how rare it is for people to combine both sets of abilities. Few philosophers can run businesses and few businesspeople have this synthetic sensibility, so necessary for good philosophy…and for actually running a business. It is Plato's "philosopher kings" who possess this rare combination of talents.

Philosophy, in contrast, is about seeing how one aspect of reality synthetically "fits" without over- or under-emphasizing other aspects, even if those aspects are the contents of other sciences. Philosophical assertions need to be balanced, and perhaps corrected and limited, by other truths (even those coming from other fields) so that we can do justice to the whole realm of being. Even if philosophy is not itself an empirical science, it ought to recognize the rightful place of the empirical in its overall understanding of reality. Something similar is needed with psychology: to bring out what it sees, but in ways that do not negate, minimize or overemphasize other truths, even if they are primarily seen and investigated by other disciplines.

Whereas an insulated analytical approach works with the natural sciences, it is questionable whether it successfully works—at least in any complete sense— for psychology, especially if it belongs to the nature of a person to be in a right relation to the world of truth, beauty and goodness. The experimental, empirical scientific method may not be necessarily the deepest and most complete approach possible towards reality. It is the most appropriate approach for some objects, such as biological, chemical and physical realities. But an exclusively empirical approach *will not even see* crucially important psychological data that is neither visible nor audible (such as our inner conscious acts).

Consider some of the benefits of integrating psychology with other disciplines: students need not only to investigate isolated subjects apart from each other, but also be able to tie insights from different fields together so that in the end, a person will have a single, comprehensive and balanced view of the world. The truths from empirical psychology will then not contradict or ignore real psychological insights coming from other fields, and those insights, in turn, will not contradict other metaphysical, ethical or religious truths coming from lived experience and other disciplines. This "delimiting"[14] of one's own field with reference to other disciplines will help our own discipline because it will help us avoid rational*ism* (as if all answers are philosophical or mathematical in nature), psycholog*ism* (as if all truths have a psychological basis) and scient*ism* (as if all truths are scientific in nature). Everyone needs to respect not just one, but all three points of view—rationality, psychology, and science—without absolutizing any one of them. Why is this important? Because truth ultimately is one, as the truth about reality does not contradict itself.

Yet, at the same time, the distinctiveness of each field also needs to be respected, insofar as psychology ought not to be obliterated by an overly rationalistic philosophy. Human motivation cannot be simply explained by an application of cold reason. Similarly, religious faith ought not to be destroyed by reducing religion either to some kind of neurosis, as Freud maintained, or reduced to mere symbolic representations of ideas for those people too unintelligent to do purely rational, metaphysical thinking, as the famous German philosopher Georg Hegel (1770-1831) held.[15]

The purpose of opening psychology to broader contexts is to do justice to those psychological truths that philosophy and other disciplines see. And it is not just the other disciplines; psychology also needs to do justice to our non-theoretical or lived psychological experience, especially if it reveals further dimensions of psychic data not given via empirically observable phenomena. For example, everyone has the experience not only of freedom but also of being "alone in our thoughts," not accessible to anyone else and even—with respect to the content[16] of one's thinking—to the most sophisticated scientific instruments.

Mainstream psychology cannot present itself as following an all-encompassing empirical, scientific method that can answer all psychological questions while at the same time asserting that one central subject matter of psychology is inner psychic acts. The empirical method—of sensible observation and inductive generalization (Chapter 6)—only works "from without," via sense perception, where the object streams in from without.[17] Any kind of "inner" conscious life—not coming in from without—is excluded from this methodology. Of course, to appreciate the scientific method as one among other methods dealing with psychological realities is fully appropriate. But that does not mean this method is appropriate for all realities having psychological significance, not only for the "inner" side of psychic acts and the conscious subject but also for morality, value, freedom, truth, person, which are similarly non-empirical phenomena (unless, of course, one tries to de-legitimize such phenomena by labeling them illusory).

Psychological texts, especially introductory ones, universally assume that *experience* and *empirical experience* are co-extensively identical. But what if this assumption—which is exactly what it is since it is never discussed by major introductory psychology texts themselves—is false? What if there are other kinds of psychological experiences that are in principle* available to us?

*THE DIFFERENCE BETWEEN SOMETHING BEING TRUE *IN PRINCIPLE* FROM BEING TRUE *IN FACT*

Consider the following examples: in principle—that is, *it belongs to the nature of*—a human being, say, to be able to understand basic mathematics. But *in fact* this is not always possible, such as if some particular person is mentally handicapped.

The notion of understanding things in principle presupposes that things have natures and that persons can come to understand them.

As I hope to show in this text, persons really do have a philosophical perception or intellectual intuition* into some things—what Plato called a seeing by "the eye of the mind"[18]—that is not reducible to sense perception (empirical intuition or observation). Employing this philosophical method will at times help psychology to properly interpret empirical, psychological data. It will be the work of this text to show that this kind of intellectual "seeing" will provide us with a rich source of psychological insight. It will be well worth the effort to get a working sense for it.

This philosophical/intellectual kind of seeing is normally implicit, and it is practically ubiquitous to everyone. Even when noticed, it is often discounted as being merely "obvious" within our (naïve) lived experience. To illustrate, consider the example of the principle of non-contradiction. It may be relatively rare for the average person to be able to properly theoretically formulate this principle (that *contradictory opposite statements cannot both be true*). But that does not mean that the average person does not have some real though implicit sense for it. Just try contradicting yourself to an attentive person with "common sense."[19] Nor does it mean that there are no hidden depths to this principle, which can be metaphysically unfolded[20] by philosophers.

*WHAT THE TERM *INTUITION* MEANS

When we use the term *intuition* colloquially, we normally mean having a kind of "sixth" sense for something. Sometimes we just have a feeling for something, even if we cannot quite express the rational basis for it. I will not use this term in that sense. Rather, I will refer to it in a technical, philosophical sense to mean a direct kind of seeing, including both empirical and intellectual. The object of this *seeing* is itself present or directly given to someone, as opposed to being merely assumed or indirectly inferred or believed.

Concerning empirical intuition, that is, referring to the various senses (seeing, hearing, touching, etc.), there is with all of them something analogous to "seeing," insofar as some kind of "object" (visible or audible phenomena, etc.) is directly given. Similarly, intellectual intuition is yet another kind of "seeing," referring to an insight into the universal nature of something.

In this text, a full, thematic presentation of "seeing with the eye of the mind" would take me too far afield.[21] There is, however, a relatively close substitute for an analysis of philosophical, intellectual intuition, and that is to take the approach of the common sense person seriously. This kind of person will see many things via their lived experience that can then be philosophically unfolded. Of course, I grant that philosophers will also say many outrageously false things not going back to any intellectual intuition, much less to common sense. Everybody faces the temptation to superimpose their own theories onto reality instead of intellectually grasping what really is the case. The claim here is not that all philosophers are always correct, but rather that intellectual intuition goes beyond any possible empirical intuition (such as, for example, that *absolutely and in principle no set of contradictory opposite statements could ever both be true*), and that this power is in principle available to everyone, albeit typically implicitly. When they do, there is a close relationship between intellectual intuition and common sense.

Naturally, a typical common sense person will not dwell on such truths in the manner of a philosopher, "clothing" (so to speak) their common sense insights with words and trying to understand their metaphysical foundation. Thus, for example, instead of saying *it belongs to the universal, strictly necessary and highly intelligible inner essence structure of x* (whatever x is) *that...*, the common sense person will rather say: *Isn't it obvious that...*(for example) *the value of a person is higher than that of a rat...that sexual slavery is immoral...that killing innocent people for racist reasons is wrong...that persons possess rational powers and reality makes sense, otherwise we would not have science...that "2+2=4"...that responsibility presupposes freedom...*, and so forth.[22] None of these assertions are empirically grounded, as there is no empirical observation or experiment that could possibly verify them in principle (or prove them false).* Nor do they *merely* go back to "common sense" either, as they are also real truths that can be investigated philosophically. One could rightly say that someone respecting them is respecting right reason. It is rational and reasonable to respect them, even if they lack an empirical warrant justifying them.

*WHY THESE TRUTHS DO NOT GO BACK TO EMPIRICAL INTUITION

One reason, among others, is that all the above assertions are universally true without exception. There is no need for statistical analysis when some true relation known by intellectual intuition applies 100% of the time, such as *responsibility presupposing freedom* and the principle of non-contradiction.

Empirical science is similarly interested in getting at universal truths, such as concerning species of plants or animals, or physical general laws. However, these truths will only be generalizations from observations of individual instances. With empirical observations into really existing, sensible individuals, there is always the possibility that a generalized knowledge of their species will yield individual variations and even exceptions, which is why statistical analysis is so important for those sciences. For example, just because all swans (in Europe) are white does not mean that *all swans are white* (as black swans exist in Australia).

In contrast, with any of the above philosophical examples (in the text paragraph above this box), exceptions are, in principle, not possible. Thus, for example, it is simply absurd to hold a non-free being, such as a rock, responsible for some action.

Of course there are times when both the philosopher and the empirical scientist will have to contradict the common sense person, such as when that person will not see deeply enough or will have insufficient knowledge. For example, imagine the sarcasm coming from the common sense person of the sixteenth century upon first hearing Copernicus' idea that it is the earth that flies around the sun instead of staying stationary. There were good reasons for this suggestion by Copernicus, but that is not to say they were evident to a level-headed, common-sense person who does not experience the movement of the earth. So there will not always be a perfect match between common sense and (philosophical and empirical) truth. But granting individual exceptions, one must tread very carefully about contradicting common sense, as a sensible person will often have more wisdom than many academics.

Consider the tremendous psychological advantage to approaching psychology, as well as everything else, from a philosophical and common-sense point of view. Both approaches emphasize *thinking for one's self,** as opposed to merely accepting theoretical positions superimposed upon lived experience. An authentic philosophical approach is all about evidence for truth and for seeing truth for one's self, as opposed to accepting assertions merely based on faith. Thus a philosopher will (or ought to) measure the datum being investigated and give only the kind and degree of assent which is rationally appropriate.

*ONE INTERESTING SIMILARITY BETWEEN VICTOR FRANKL AND SOCRATES

When Victor Frankl (1905-1997) applies his logotherapeutic[23] techniques, he is aware of the importance of the clients finding their own meaning. It is not enough for the client to hear something true; they as persons also need to "see" this truth *for themselves.*

In this way, Frankl is similar to the great philosopher Socrates, who, with his philosophical deliberations with others, steadfastly refused to give "answers," but rather insisted that his interlocutors discover truth in dialogue (or discussion) where they could come to see some truth for themselves. As with Socrates, it will not do for Frankl to have clients simply accept what some therapist thinks is true without seeing for themselves, even if it really is in fact true. To badger a client into accepting what he doesn't see, Frankl identifies as an instance of "countertransference," as when a therapist successfully forces his own ideas or feelings on to another in therapy without that client making those ideas "his (or her) own." This approach is both philosophically and psychologically counterproductive.

It is worth emphasizing that this "personalistic concern" for the client as an independent thinker in no way implies any kind of relativism, as if each person has "their own meaning and reality." No, both Socrates and Frankl are interested in other people thinking what is actually true. It just needs to be accomplished respectfully, where this integration of truth with the person is complete.

As attractive as this scenario of thinking for one's self is, there is an important qualification. Concerning the empirical sciences, there is often a role (especially for introductory students) for taking things on a kind of faith. I am not thinking here of religious faith, but rather to a faith or trust that should be appropriately given to empirically oriented texts from reputable sources, including both introductory science and psychology texts. It makes sense to give these vetted authorities a certain credit, even before students have a chance to replicate those empirical findings on their own.[24] Even if one never replicates for one's self most empirical findings (obviously the sheer volume of the research makes this impossible), it is still reasonable to give serious, reputable scientists a kind of "credit of faith." But, this "credit" only applies if their interpretations stay within the reasonable bounds of the actual empirical evidence (while, at the same time, being wary of scientists who can and do abuse their authority by making what is in effect merely ideological, political or culturally acceptable assertions under the guise of science). In contrast, students of philosophy—including those new to the field—ought to insist on evidence beyond taking somebody's word for things, even from reputable authorities.

Why is that? It is worthwhile understanding this difference between philosophy and the empirical sciences. The reason for trusting reputable empirical authorities is because the natural sciences will quickly go beyond our normal lived experience, going back to specialized observations, often using sophisticated instruments. Here there is a source of knowledge not available to the (non-scientist) common sense person. In contrast, philosophers—simply as a point of fact—do not make specialized observations or use scientific instruments that would give them a different, unique experience unavailable to our naive experience. The source of their experience is our *common* lived experience of reality, grounded in natural reason,* which then in principle can be verified by others. This "common" experience is only one aspect of an individual person's total experience, which can include other experiences, such as, perhaps, inner conscious experiences, or a religious revelation given to some but not to others.

*NATURAL REASON

That which is given via "natural reason" is in principle open to everyone. This point can be clearly seen by considering two contrasting examples from ethics.

Let us say, for the sake of the argument, that God commands someone (or a people) not to eat pork. Here it is obvious that in order for someone to know about this prohibition, God has to first make it known (promulgation). Why? Because no one could just "figure this prohibition out" because, well, there is nothing intrinsically wrong with eating pork. But just as parents have the right to legitimately command something in itself neutral to children (*make your bed!*), so perhaps God has that right too.

Now contrast the above example with that of, say, someone torturing and killing an innocent person for racist reasons. You no doubt would rightly say that such an action is in itself horrendous and evil. Seeing its wrongness is clearly not dependent upon anybody's command and subsequent promulgation. Believers and atheists both see it.

While the first example (*don't eat pork!*) presupposes some kind of revelation, insight into the wrongness of the second action (*murdering people for racist reasons*) simply goes back to natural reason, referring to a seeing that is "in principle" common to everyone. This does not mean that in fact everyone automatically sees it. There are people who are so blinded by their own racism and cruelty that they do not in fact see it. Thus, our "common natural reason" refers to the fact that everyone (in principle) can and should see it, with some level of responsibility for not seeing it.

It is not just ethical principles that go back to natural reason, but metaphysical principles as well, such as the principle of contradiction. In fact, all of philosophy and mathematics in principle goes back to natural reason, as opposed to any kind of some special revelation given to some and not to others, even though not everyone in fact can adequately grasp and articulate them.

Even though empirical scientists will typically have a source of knowledge not given to non-researchers, there is a sense in which the empirical findings of one researcher are open to being verified by other scientists (Chapter 2). So, in this sense natural science has to be open in principle to everyone, even if it is true in fact that there is often a source of knowledge that is not given in our naïve lived experience.

In contrast, with philosophy there is no "special" or "secret" experience or source of knowledge open, somehow, to the professional that is not in principle open to the novice. Naturally, there are "layers" of experience, and a great philosopher will often take us to our depth where, perhaps, we have been too superficial before. The point is that this "depth" is in principle available to all of us in experience, even when we do not in fact actualize it.

In the next chapter, I will investigate psychological phenomena where this factor of being "common to many" is missing, where crucially important psychological content is only given to us individually. For example, my inner life is only given to me as your conscious life is only given to you. This fact will pose a serious challenge to the idea the psychology is an exclusively empirical science because the natural sciences, like philosophy, presuppose common accessibility to data.

Chapter 2

Psychological Empiricism (Part A): Do Non-Empirical Psychological Phenomena Exist?

One central starting point of mainline introductory psychology texts is that the exclusive mode of investigation is the empirical method.[25] In this chapter, I want to test that idea by looking for phenomena that are both non-empirical as well as being clearly important for the discipline of psychology. If such data can be found, they will constitute a good argument against psychological empiric*ism* and the exclusive use of the empirical method.* An investigation of the proper starting points for psychology will be the topic of Chapters 4 and 5, as I want to investigate the appropriate subject matter of psychology. In Chapter 3, four arguments against a strict empiricist psychological approach will be given, as well as one possible explanation for why contemporary psychology is today so dominated by empiricism. It is worth mentioning again that one can be completely against psychological empiric*ism* while endorsing the truth that many questions of psychology can only be explored empirically.

*METHOD HAS TO FOLLOW CONTENT, NOT VICE VERSA

The temptation for contemporary psychology is to *simply assert* that the only suitable object of psychological investigation concerns that which is empirically verifiable because, after all, the empirical sciences include psychology. If this circular reasoning is uncritically accepted, then it becomes easy to simply ignore all instances of non-empirical psychological data. But this claim puts the cart before the horse, insofar as one's method should not determine content. For example, it makes no sense to insist on studying colors by the exclusive method of hearing or sounds by seeing. If a reality is only visible, then we obviously need to look, not listen. Thus, one needs to first investigate the nature of the subject matter to be studied, and then find the method most appropriate to that content. It is only after clarifying the object to be studied that one can subsequently look for a suitable method for investigating it.

Two phenomena that are both psychological and non-empirical will be investigated in this chapter. The first is the whole realm of "inner" conscious experience, and the second concerns intrinsic value. Both go back to and are grounded in our lived experience of reality (Chapter 1), thereby being open to philosophical investigation, and not to some special experience given via scientific instrumentation.

Every person possesses the power of an inner conscious life, which can be philosophically investigated.* Perhaps there are times in which we do not experience it, such as when we are in a dreamless sleep or coma. Thus, there is a distinction between the *power* to think or will or be conscious from the *exercise* of those powers. The powers are grounded in our basic personal nature as human beings,[26] while the exercise of those powers depends on many other factors (such as biochemistry, brain temperature, etc.).

*HOW CAN THE "PRIVACY" OF INNER CONSCIOUS EXPERIENCE BE STUDIED PHILOSOPHICALLY?

In the last chapter, one condition was noted for the possibility of an object being studied philosophically is that it be open to our common, lived experience. Now I can add that our individual, inner experience is open only to each person's own experience and not to others (unless, of course, we tell others about what is going on inside of us) and that conscious life is open to philosophical investigation. This may seem to the attentive reader to be contradictory.

In response, one could say that my experience *as mine* is not a suitable object of philosophical reflection. But, certainly, the general or universal idea that every person (in principle) possesses the power of an inner, conscious life is a suitable object of philosophical reflection.

Conscious experience is an utterly necessary condition for the very possibility of a science of psychology. Without conscious life, there is no psychology. There could be behavior, but behavior alone without consciousness can refer to anything, for all living and even non-living beings *behave*. Furthermore, persons are by their very nature built for an inner conscious life. If for some reason they cannot actualize that life, they will not be able to fulfill their nature, which requires loving, willing, thinking, and so forth. These are all conscious acts.

What is this inner, personal conscious life? Everyone knows what it is like to be alone with their own thoughts. No doubt there have been situations where we felt uncomfortable sharing our thoughts frankly with others. Maybe I am politically a Democrat in a room full of Republicans, or vice versa. In such conversations, I might sympathetically smile at those people, yet I keep my own opinions to myself. Notice when this is successfully done, no one is the wiser—unless of course I happen to betray myself via bodily expression or behavior—for no one else has a direct admission to our own inner life. My inner life is for me alone; yours is for you alone.

Now contrast this inner subjective experience with objects given via sense perception, especially from the senses of seeing and hearing. These sensed objects, of course, are open to many people (granting differences of perspective). They are obviously not given as private, and they follow certain patterns of behavior, making them predictable. Even if aspects of empirical experience are only open to scientists—insofar as only they will have access to scientific instrumentation and expertise not available to others—there remains with them a potentiality for a certain common experience with other scientists, which is important for replication of experiments for the scientific method.[27] For example, the scientific "breakthrough" in the 1980s of cold fusion could not be repeated. The condition for the possibility of science is that empirical experience must be in principle common to those who possess the resources and knowledge to replicate this experience. It is exactly this condition that is missing with our inner, individual conscious experience.

Objects given via sense perception and inner conscious experience are two very different kinds and dimensions of conscious experience. I do not observe my own thoughts "from without," as if they are objects "out there," over against me. I rather experience and perform them "from within," as both psychic acts and the conscious personal self are inwardly given. In contrast, I observe objects of the senses existing "from without," in the real world. And these observations then become verifiable by similar observations from others, giving here the possibility of a commonality of perception. But our own thoughts, which are only on the "inside" and are not directly accessible to others, are only accessible to ourselves.

Not only are my thoughts on the "inside," my own self is given to me on the "inside" as well, for, after all, it is "I" who am conscious. To try to explain the phenomena of my own inner life exclusively through perception (as if I have to perceive myself to be aware of myself) is to affect a weird kind of alienation from myself, as if my own thoughts have to be somehow sensed "over against" me, "out there" separated from me.* But I do not perceive my own thoughts outside of myself; I rather consciously perform them from within (Chapter 4). They are mine insofar as I possess myself. Since I am not you and you are not me, only I can have my own inner experience, and you yours.

*SELF-ALIENATION IN B. F. SKINNER

B. F. Skinner is one example of a thinker whose theory does not acknowledge self-presence (that is, my "self" and my conscious acts as "inside"), and instead wants to explain our knowledge of ourselves in terms of a perception, as if we get at our self only "from without." For example, he states, "that the inner man seems at times to be directly observed. We must infer the jubilance of a falling body, but can we not feel our own jubilance? We do, indeed, feel things inside our own skin, but we do not feel the things which have been invented [such as the notion of the "autonomous man"] to explain behavior."[28]

Notice in the above quote Skinner admits to an inner conscious life ["feel[ing] things inside our own skin"]. But does not admit to being present to his own self as the one feeling them. Thus, he adopts in effect a position of self-alienation from his own self, as if we only observe—from without—ourselves perceiving or promising or getting angry.

Besides this privacy of our own individual psychic life, there is a second evidence for the non-empirical nature of this inner, conscious life: they lack the empirical (sensible and material) predicates (or properties) that everything material must possess. For example, being gaseous or liquid, circular or rectangular, being three or four or five inches or feet in length, weighing so many ounces or pounds, in no way characterizes this inner conscious life. Naturally, something can be material without having any specific one of these kinds of properties. But they must have some of them, and if any individual thing has even one, it is thereby confirmed as being material in nature. In contrast, our inner acts of loving or willing are not colored or gaseous. They are not so many inches long or high, weighing three pounds or four, nor do they have any other kind of optional material (or empirical, sensible) predicate. Nor does the personal self who performs these acts possess any of these material properties.* Since not everything material will have any particular one of these kinds of properties, they are "optional." But if neither psychic acts nor the personal self who performs these acts possess any of these optional material properties, it doesn't really make sense to think of these phenomena as being material in nature.

AN OBJECTION: ARE NOT PERSONS EMBODIED?

The claim of the above text is that no material or empirical properties are applicable to the personal self. Later on, this observation will be my evidence for a distinction between body and soul (Chapter 6).

But a reasonable objection is that the personal self has to be material because it is in union with and immersed in a material body. Since the body is material, the personal self has to be embodied as well. Because we are body-soul composite beings, it seems a mere abstraction to talk about the being of the personal self as immaterial.

I grant that the personal self is embodied in the sense of forming a body/soul composite being. We are body-soul beings. If someone does not respect their own or someone else's body, they are not respecting their person. But there is a real sense in which it is legitimate to consider the possibility of the soul existing as separated from its body, at least insofar as many religious traditions maintain that the soul can and will survive the death of its body (establishing the truth or falsity of this point is not here my business). Even among non-believers, there might be a surprisingly large number who think they will somehow survive the death of their body.

Furthermore, even within the body-soul composite being the personal self maintains a certain relative distinction from the body, a difference within unity, despite the mutual immersion of body and soul. Given this distinction, it then becomes possible to evaluate the soul simply on its own terms (Chapter 4) and in its own nature.

Notice this too: unless you are willing to go the route of some kind of radical behaviorism where the object of psychology is exclusively behavior and explicitly not inner psychic experiences, you cannot deny the reality or the significance of these inner psychic acts and conscious being. They are too clearly and obviously given in our lived experience. In fact, they form the very heart of psychology (Chapter 5).

The second non-empirical datum possessing psychological significance is **value**, by which I mean specifically and exclusively *intrinsic value** or what is objectively important-in-itself, independent of what anybody else thinks or feels. For example, the insight is clearly available—unless someone is prejudiced by something like racial or class-based ideologies—that all persons, by their very human nature, are beings possessing a high intrinsic importance. This insight obtains even while granting that some persons can be highly immoral. But even immoral persons are persons, and as such, deserve a basic respect given to persons.

*TWO MEANINGS OF THE WORD *VALUE*: THE PHILOSOPHICAL,
TECHNICAL MEANING VERSUS THE COLLOQUIAL SENSE

In this text, the term *value* will be used exclusively in a technical,
philosophical sense to mean that which is *intrinsically important* or
what is *important-in-itself.* More exactly, value refers to an intrinsic and
fully objective property (or attribute) of a being, which makes that being
important-in-itself.

In the English language, the term *value* typically refers—in a different
sense of the term—to simply what is *important to someone.* In this
second, colloquial meaning, value can refer to both what is objectively
important-in-itself *and* to what subjectively gives someone pleasure.
This second meaning (value=objective and subjective importance) is a
perfectly legitimate use of the term. It is just not the sense I will use in
this text.

It is important to stress that in this text the term *value* will be exclusively
used in the above first sense (value=intrinsic importance). Thus, in this
text, *value* and *intrinsic value* are synonymous.

One reason why this notion of value is of interest to psychology is because of
its link to motivation. It is a basic law of motivation that it takes something
important to motivate a person.[29] Since values are intrinsically important, they
can motivate a person. Psychology is clearly interested in motivation.
Furthermore, values can be found either as properties of beings (such as
persons) or of psychic acts performed by persons (such as just or loving acts),
and these acts—because they are psychic in nature—are of interest to
psychology. On the other hand, since values really exist either as fully objective
properties of beings (and psychic acts), they also have a kind of independence
from psychology, insofar as they are not merely a product of any psychic act of
"valuing," as if by that act I give you "value."[30] This would subjectivize value.

Whereas value refers to a kind of importance that is intrinsic to a being, there
is another kind of importance, which is called the importance of the
subjectively satisfying.[31] This kind of importance is motivated—not by the
intrinsic importance of an object—but by one's anticipated subjective pleasure,
such as the pleasure of drinking a cold Pepsi on a hot day.

Both pleasure and displeasure (of what is subjectively satisfying or
dissatisfying) are instances of two kinds of appearance.* Thus, for example, a
Pepsi appears to me differently when I am hot and thirsty than when I am not.
Appearances refer to a subjective aspect of something, like the goodness of a

Pepsi. In contrast, there is no subjective contribution to the being of value, as value is already intrinsic to the being possessing the value.

*APPEARANCES

An appearance is neither a thing nor a fully objective property of a thing (like extendedness in material beings). It is the way things present themselves in relation to us. Appearances are relational realities, and thus are not intrinsic to the being that bears them. Big and small, fast and slow, colors and sounds, pleasurable and unpleasurable are all examples of appearances. Both appearances and illusions have a kind of subjective and relational reality in the sense of being either partial (appearances) or complete (illusions) products of psychic acts. As such, they are dependent upon our subjectivity. But things such as cars and mountains and other persons are not psychic realities. They are rather things-in-themselves having a kind of being independent of our subjectivity. Values, of course, are also not things, but fully objective properties of things. Because values are fully objective in nature, they do not have the kind of being of either an appearance or an illusion.

Cars and mountains and other persons exist "in themselves," not as properties of things—like values—but as things-in-themselves (substances). Neither substances nor intrinsic value are experienced as having a kind of being that is dependent upon our subjectivity. For example, you do not exist at the mercy of my perceiving you, even though it is true that an appearance (such as seeing you *as small* from a distance) only exists at the mercy of my perceiving you. Something similar can be said about intrinsic value. A person in fact possesses intrinsic value independent of what anybody thinks, even though to a racist, a Jew or black may appear as worthless.

Notice that things can appear to us via our senses, but the thing that appears is obviously not an appearance. It is rather a being existing in itself, via a certain perspectivity. Thus, a mountain appears big when we are close to it, but small when we see it from space. The qualities of big and small are appearances. However, appearances do not appear; it is things-in-themselves that appear. The mountain is not an appearance, but a being existing-in-itself that appears. Thus, our psychic perception of the mountain is that of a combination of both subjective and objective factors: the subjective factor going back to perspectivity (big and small, fast or slow, etc.) as well as our particular biological constitution (colors[32] and sounds), and the objective factor going back to the thing-in-itself that appears.

Since appearances (and illusions) have a kind of psychic reality, they will be of interest to psychology. My claim is that the being of a value is not reducible to an appearance. Just as mountains and persons can appear without their being reduced to appearances, so can values—as a property of a being making that being important-in-itself—appear as well in various ways, even though they too are not mere appearances.

One might think I may be philosophically nitpicking here with the distinction between an appearance and a thing that appears, but notice that if someone collapses that distinction, everything then becomes in effect an appearance. This is one version of idealism, where everything is measured by the way they appear to us. Then all of reality becomes dependent upon and relative to my own acts of perceiving, and "to be is to be perceived,"[33] as the philosopher Bishop George Berkeley (1685-1753) puts it. Another version of idealism is with value relativism, where values are reducible merely to what someone thinks is important. In both versions, *appearances swallow up things-in-themselves*, and we are now cut off from knowing and responding to reality as it is in itself.

Values, therefore, are not appearances as they exist completely on the object side, "out there" so to speak, in reality. Thus, I do not give you "value," I rather discover it. It pre-exists any psychic attitude of mine or anyone else. I recognize it, I find it. I do not create it. If I did create it (or "make it up"), I could theoretically then take it away. It would then not be "intrinsic" at all, but relational or relative to me or to us.

These two kinds of importance, value and the pleasure of the subjectively satisfying, are experienced differently. With value, one can sense a "call" or an "ought"[34] to respect the being possessing the value encountered in some concrete situation. These "calls" obviously do not refer to any literal calling, using language. Rather, when someone encounters a being and recognizes its intrinsic value, there goes with that recognition also a kind of invitation to respect it. All values do this. With these "oughts," there is something rational, sober, quiet, and respectful to our freedom, which is no doubt one reason why they are so easy to ignore.

Thus, there are two very different kinds of importance: the importance of value, which exists as a fully objective property of some thing or act, and the importance of pleasure (or the subjectively satisfying),[35] which is clearly dependent upon or relational to our subjectivity, specifically to our pleasure.

Persons are important in themselves, and not merely because of the pleasure they can give me.

Not only are values non-psychological, they are also non-empirical as well. For the value of a person is not so many inches long or gaseous or rectangular. None of these material properties, which were noticed before as applying material things but not to psychic acts, are applicable to values. Thus, values are non-sensible. They are not grasped by our literal senses, but rather by "the eye of the mind," as Plato puts it.

Intrinsic value is important for psychology for the following five reasons.

First, while value as fully objective property of things is independent of psychology insofar as it is not itself a product of a psychic act of "valuing" something, it remains related to psychology insofar as it can be an objective property of psychic acts. Psychic acts, such as loving and willing, are of primary importance to psychology, and they can be important-in-themselves. Thus, for instance, the risk taken out of love to try to save someone's life in a dangerous situation is a great value in and of itself.

Second, our power to recognize the world of value reveals something about our nature as its being distinctly personal. Causal events happen in nature, and animals can respond by instinctual desire to what gives them pleasure, but only persons can perceive and respond to that which is important-in-itself. While animal affection for their loving masters can mimic personal love, only persons can give a value response. Why? Because values cannot be grasped by any of the five senses—which animals can possess—but only by the "eye of the mind," or in other words, by a personal act of understanding what it is that one perceives, which animals do not possess. Love is essentially value responding, and animals cannot grasp values. Certainly, animals can respond to beings possessing intrinsic values, but only persons can respond to a value *as a value*.

Third, while value is not itself a psychic reality, it is one kind of motivation, and motivation is certainly an important subject of psychological inquiry. It is of course not the only kind of motivation as we are often moved by our own self-interest and pleasure.* It is one thing to say that we are typically motivated by pleasure, and it is quite another to say that it is the only kind of motivation, thereby denying or at least ignoring value as a further kind of motivation.

*DISTINGUISHING THE INNOCENT LURE OF THE SUBJECTIVELY SATISFYING FROM FRANK TEMPTATIONS

Sometimes people will consider all pleasures, especially bodily pleasures, as evil. But how could the pleasure of drinking something like a Pepsi be evil?

What then distinguishes innocent from tempting urges? With the example of the Pepsi, what explains this enticing is clearly our need for hydration and our desire for pleasure. And of course this desire is completely innocent and legitimate.

Consider, however, other instances of the enticing quality of the subjectively satisfying that are far less innocent, which involve an ignoring or even a destruction of a high value for the sake of the subjectively satisfying enjoyment of something. For example, there is nothing wrong with someone wanting to be king, but there is something wrong with willing to murder for the sake of becoming king. The criterion for illicit pleasures: does the pleasure involve the ignoring or the destruction of beings possessing high value?

Sometimes these two kinds of motivation—value and the subjectively satisfying (pleasure)—can be confused. Someone could fool himself into thinking he is motivated by (the value of) justice, when he in fact he is merely "dressing up" his lust for revenge by using the language of justice. Or, alternatively, both kinds of motivation can also become blended together, making the value response (again, of wanting justice) be partially infected by a subjectively satisfying desire (for revenge), having the effect of making the value response impure. Psychologists can be rightly suspicious of someone's self-proclaimed interest in justice, insofar as people can obviously be influenced by baser motivations, even without realizing it. On the other hand, psychologists also need to be careful to avoid cynicism. Sometimes a person is really serious about respecting some high value for its own sake, sometimes even to the point of preferring death to betraying it.

Furthermore, a response to what is intrinsically precious in itself can also go in tandem with the pleasure of simply following our instincts.[36] A mother, for instance, could give her child presents out of both love for her child (value motivation) and out of a motherly instinct. Or, a person can act against his instincts, such as ignoring his own preservation of life instinct for the sake of risking his life out of love to save another. Animals too will sacrifice their life for their families (including their human families, if they are pets), but this sacrifice seems to be out of its instinctual nature (preservation of the species)—or at least out of its strongest instinct—and certainly not from any rational understanding of intrinsic value (insofar as animals lack the rational, personal power to perceive values). Animals will never go against their own instincts.

Freud has an interesting way of combining these two kinds of motivation through what he calls *sublimation*. This psycho-analytic term refers to the phenomenon of transferring a certain instinctual, sexual energy to interests and projects that are more socially acceptable, especially important in those situations where a person lacks the power to simply take the object of one's pleasure. In this way, some aspect of pleasure will still be experienced, even if it is disguised by being displaced by some socially acceptable good or "value." Freud attempted to explain all morality and even all value motivation in this way. Thus, in sublimation, a person is not really responding to a being possessing an intrinsic value for its own sake, but rather to something insofar as it yields displaced (sexual) pleasure. This interpretation in effect psychologizes all value motivation, reducing it to the level of the subjectively satisfying. Then the ultimate basis for all value motivation is sublimated pleasure as opposed to responding adequately to the being possessing the value for its own sake. For example, a person may become an artist, not for the sake of celebrating beauty, but rather as a socially acceptable outlet for expressing one's own sexualized energy.

Certainly, one can grant that sublimation occurs while at the same time recognizing that individuals can also be authentically motivated by what is genuinely beautiful and loving. To reduce all motivation simply to variations of a sublimated instinct gratification is in effect reducing human motivation to the level of the subjectively satisfying.

Fourth, while values themselves are intrinsic to the beings that bear them and thus not dependent for their existence upon our subjectivity (specifically, our pleasure), various kinds of counterfeits of value really are dependent upon our subjectivity and are thereby of central interest to psychology. Consider some of the different kinds of counterfeits: virtue signaling (bragging about how virtuous one is), scapegoating, and ressentiment,* which then can lead to value blindness. All are of great psychological interest. But they are far more difficult to even identify, much less explain, unless they are first seen as perversions in the intellectual "light" of authentic value. For just as injustice only becomes intelligible in relation to justice (as injustice is essentially an "attack" upon what is just), so these perversions become properly identifiable only in the light of authentic value.

*RESSENTIMENT

While value blindness, scapegoating and blunting of conscience can be philosophically and psychologically unfolded, practically everyone has a pre-theoretical sense for them simply from their lived experience. Ressentiment, however, is more difficult to detect. Even though this is a French term, it refers to a psychological phenomenon that is everywhere. The philosophers Friedrich Nietzsche (1844-1900) and Max

Scheler (1874-1928) identified and analyzed this phenomenon. Scheler describes it in this way,

> Ressentiment is a self-poisoning of the mind which has quite definite causes and consequences. It is a lasting mental attitude, caused by the systematic repression of certain emotions and affects which, as such, are normal components of human nature. Their repression leads to the constant tendency to indulge in certain kinds of value delusions and corresponding value judgments. The emotions and affects primarily concerned are revenge, hatred, malice, envy, the impulse to detract, and spite.[37]

Although all the above emotions are "gateways" to resentment, consider as an example envy. Imagine someone in a superior position, whether in terms of position, physical strength, popularity or talent. This superiority may lead me to envy, which in turn motivates dislike (it is, after all, unfair that I do not have his talent or position) and the finding of fault to justify the dislike. If the other is somehow powerful, any expression of dislike could be dangerous. So, instead of simply reacting outward against the other, projecting out psychological anger and venom, thereby dissipating it, my envy is rather inwardly repressed and will be expressed in a disguised form.

What better way to "get back"—in a surreptitious way—than to have "pity" towards that other. The superior other is now interpreted not as strong, but as pathetic. And then this way of thinking will tend to spread out to other instances: instead of appreciating the value of strength, weakness is glorified; and instead of wealth, poverty is exalted. This is how Nietzsche explains all value and morality, especially Christian morality. Such Christian values (such as mercy, forgiveness, charity, etc.) are for him nothing but an expression of this resentment attitude, the fruit of this psychological mechanism leading to what Nietzsche calls the "falsification of the value tablets."[38]

Scheler sees the irony with this last claim, insofar as authentic values have to first exist in order for them to be falsified. If that is true, then all value cannot be reducible to and explained by ressentiment—as Nietzsche claimed—insofar as ressentiment itself presupposes value, which it then perverts.

It is very helpful to clearly distinguish two phenomena: intrinsic value from these cheap imitations of it. For example, what is it that the psychologist is trying to explain: intrinsic value or one of these imitations? Distinguishing them without reducing them to authentic value would be quite helpful.

Fifth, psychology deals not only with mental dysfunction, but also what leads to authenticity and to what genuinely fulfills persons. One criterion for authenticity is to be "real" in the sense of being in a right relation to the world. If it is true that values are part of "the objective furniture of the world," that is, objective properties of beings as they are in themselves, then to be in a right relation to truth *and* intrinsic goodness is in that sense to be real and authentic.

Two levels of authenticity can be distinguished. The first refers to people knowing their own mind and feelings—being true to themselves—as opposed to confusing their wants and interests with someone else's. A radical form of this confusion is what psychologists call *introjection*, where they not only automatically assent but even confuse their own thinking, willing and feeling with someone else's.[39] Perhaps such people have been cowed in their life by an overwhelmingly powerful and threatening other (such as an abusive father figure), and so to adopt the feelings and attitudes of that person will be a safety mechanism. However, for adults[40] to make this confusion is to be profoundly inauthentic. In contrast, an authentic person will have the courage to know his or her own mind and feelings, and then will stand up for them.

As legitimate as this first level is, for someone to successfully resist the opinions of others and to think and to will for one's own self does not by itself distinguish a mature person from a psychopath. Psychopaths could very well also know their own mind, act in their own name, and simultaneously not care about external influences, including what is authentically good and true. With the example of a psychopath in mind, it becomes clear that something else is needed, a second level of authenticity. This second level refers not merely to subjectively "knowing one's own mind" and "acting in one's own name," but also making the effort to conform one's life to what is authentically good and true, especially to the world of intrinsic value.* The psychopath is completely uninterested in what is authentically good and true, even if he does know his own mind.

*WHAT IF A PERSON'S WILL IS CONSTRAINED BY WHAT IS GOOD AND TRUE?

Could one pit the first and the second levels of authenticity against one another? If so, would it be inauthentic to go against one's own will and desires to bow to what is morally good? Should not persons be true to themselves?

Carl Rogers gives an example of someone emphasizing the first level at the expense of the second when he approvingly quotes one of his clients to say, "I've always felt I had to do things because they were expected of me, or more important, to make people like me. The hell with it! I think from now on I'm going to just be me—rich or poor, good or bad, rational or irrational, logical or illogical, famous or infamous."[41] It seems obvious that morality can inhibit our will and desires, leading to inner psychological conflict.

In response, at the deepest level, I do not think there is any contradiction between the first and second levels because to ignore what is authentically good *in the name of freedom* actually leads in short order to a loss of freedom. For example, everyone knows—if they pay attention—that the more they give in to their own addictions and vices, the stronger they become. And the stronger they are, the less freedom those people will have.

The same point can be made with a positive example. Notice how our freedom increases to the degree that we come more and more into a right relation to the world of value and goodness. For example, someone who is generous will be freer to exercise their generosity than someone else who is constricted and cramped by their own selfishness. This second kind of person could in principle be generous in some action by a cold act of will, but it will be painful and difficult, especially compared to the ease of the generous person acting generously.

While granting the experience of Rogers' client, perhaps that person needs to see his situation from a deeper point of view, which reveals no ultimate contradiction between these two levels of authenticity.

While the first level of authenticity is important, it also seems to be a rather low bar. In contrast, notice how persons actualize themselves in a deeper way when they love, which then leads to self-discovery. Persons who love find their true selves. The noise and distractions surrounding us in daily life suddenly fall away, the superficialities of life become identified with only the center remaining.*

*TWO DISTINCT SOURCES OF SELF-KNOWLEDGE

Everyone, for example, knows the beautiful Disney cartoon rendition of the fairy tale, *The Beauty and the Beast*, of how the Beast will forever remain a beast...until he can learn how to love. There is psychological truth to this story because as long as he lives only for himself in the immanent[42] cocoon of his own pleasures and instincts, even if he knows his own feelings and thinking (the first level of authenticity), he will still forever remain a beast. It is only when he comes to love Belle that he discovers himself as he really is, a prince. Thus, for instance, the Beast—in loving Belle and having that love requited—discovers he is not a beast at all, but a prince.

The kind of insight the Beast has is a real, though unreflective self-knowledge. Normally, we think of self-knowledge as only referring to self-reflection, either alone or with the help of another, including of course with professional counselors. Self-reflection is an utterly crucial form of self-knowledge, but it is not the only kind, as the self-knowledge displayed by the Beast is hardly a product of self-reflection at all (Chapter 3). It rather results from a deepening of one's self by being "touched" by some high value. It seems that the Beast actualizes a deeper center within himself when he falls in love with Belle, even without self-reflection. Yet, this love still leads to the self-discovery that he is actually a prince.

The topic of intrinsic value is important. Yet, contemporary psychology could easily miss this datum, at least in some explicit theoretical way, when it insists upon its own empirical pedigree. Strict empiricism can certainly miss this datum, but the reality of value remains so ubiquitous that it is hard to be consistent. For example, the *American Psychological Association* (APA), despite its stated single-minded reliance on the empirical nature of psychology, implies or at least presupposes the datum of intrinsic value when it rightly states, "Psychologists respect the dignity and worth of all people...."[43]

One wonders, where do these notions of "dignity and worth" come from? What is it that justifies them? Is this an idea the APA just "makes up" out of thin air, or is there some kind of rational ground or basis justifying it? Has it been empirically observed? If so, it should then be open to being empirically measured or weighed, thereby fitting into their own methodology. There is, however, no such empirical measure because empirical facts only deal with *what is the case*, while value refers to *what is intrinsically good* and *what ought to be*.

With the reality and being of value, as an intrinsic property of beings, there is an answer to what it is that grounds this dignity: it is the intrinsic value "of each individual person."

Chapter 3

Psychological Empiricism (Part B): A Critique

In the last chapter, two non-empirical realities were investigated—inner conscious experience and intrinsic value—whose psychological significance challenges contemporary psychology's claim to be an exclusively empirical science. This chapter explores four further reasons why a purely psychological empiricism is problematic, and then gives a theory as to why mainline psychology has become dominated by an exclusively empirical point of view.

The first point is this: if it is true that psychology is entirely empirical in nature, it would follow that only empirical scientists should adjudicate all psychological questions.

It is worth asking whether the opinions of the scientists and the scientific approach can judge such phenomena as a person's inner conscious states, experiences of intrinsic value or basic metaphysical principles, which are so completely outside their own domain of sensible, empirical data. It is unnecessary to assume some anti-scientific attitude when claiming that science cannot resolve *all* questions, including many psychological questions. One can grant that concerning some psychological questions—such as childhood development, the classification of different mental illnesses, learning theory, neuropsychology, and so forth—it is completely appropriate to take the findings and opinions of reputable scientists seriously.

Still, one wonders how psychologically healthy it is to let the "experts" do our thinking for us concerning all psychological questions, especially if it is not true that every psychological datum is empirical in nature. It is one thing when scientists have a source of knowledge not given to me, because then they will have experiences and data I lack. But concerning non-empirical, philosophically oriented psychological phenomena, they are on the same level as me. Of course they might be smarter or wiser than me, so I need to be open to their arguments. We can all learn from each other. But they do not have any special source of insight that I lack. If their assertions are really philosophical in nature, I need to see their arguments and justifications. For, after all, belief is not part of the methodology of philosophy, even for beginners. And any appeal to authority dealing with philosophy or the non-empirical dimensions of psychology is similarly insufficient and inappropriate (Chapter 1). This is especially the case when one sees that part of growing up and maturing as a person is to learn to think for one's self.

Secondly, psychological empiric*ism* is reductionistic in the sense of inevitably leading thinkers to explain higher realities in terms of the lower ones, especially with those psychological issues like moral, metaphysical and religious concerns.

Before explaining and justifying this second point, it might be helpful to first note those times in which an apparently reductionistic account really is an appropriate explanation, insofar as what at times goes by the name of goodness, morality, and truth can often be rather less than advertised. Everyone knows of politicians who merely pander to people's base desires and prejudices, and yet are really motivated by their own interests. Sometimes these politicians are aware that they are self-consciously lying to people, and sometimes they even fool themselves by actually believing their own drivel.* But, if the truth be told, it is not necessary to look at anyone else, as we can at times see this very same tendency to "dress up" our own motivations in ourselves. In fact, it might be a bad sign if we never notice this inclination in ourselves, as it suggests an insufficiency of awareness of this rather ubiquitous human tendency.

*ARISTOTLE'S ILLUMINATING DISTINCTION BETWEEN "INCONTINENT" AND "INTEMPERATE" PERSONS

In the *Nicomachean Ethics* (Book 7, Chapter 7), Aristotle (383-320 BC) makes an interesting psychological/ethical distinction between incontinence and intemperance. The incontinent man knowingly does wrong. He is going against his better judgement and he knows it, typically leading to an inward psychological conflict. On some level, this person wants what is authentically just and good, but he wants to gratify his instincts as well. So, in his weakness he wills his pleasure over what is just. Thus, there is inner conflict.

In contrast, the intemperate man's injustice has grown so great that he is blinded to his own evil, with the result being that inner conflict is largely or completely absent. This kind of blindness, however, is one for which he is responsible because he has freely performed those actions, which, in turn, have led to blindness. The incontinent man's character has not yet devolved into that kind of value blindness. He still possesses some insight. The intemperate man is more confirmed in his evil than the incontinent person since he doesn't even recognize his actions as evil anymore.

Practically everyone can relate the above to the following simple observation: the first time someone steals, he will typically feel guilty and ashamed. By the tenth time? Not so much. But by the hundredth time: hey, this guy thinks he is a businessman.

It is an instance of simple realism to see the times in which we all fool ourselves into thinking we are better than we really are. But saying that *all* people at *all* times are exclusively motivated by baser motives and that all goodness is just a sham is reductionistic cynicism.

B. F. Skinner's behaviorism is one example of such a reductionistic approach. He attempts to explain a person's value response motivation completely in terms of his principles of conditioning.[44] Skinner is a radical behaviorist, and the whole idea of a moral order has no place in his empiricistic worldview of neutral facts. He explains the psychological experience of moral guilt with this example: "Consider a young man whose world has suddenly changed…he feels guilty or ashamed (*he has previously been punished for idleness or failure, which now evokes emotional responses*)."[45] Skinner's interpretation of the young man's motive, which he italicizes, is certainly one possible ground of someone's feeling of something approximating guilt, but this kind of explanation does not explain authentic moral guilt. Genuine guilt has to be motivated by a violation of something understood as genuinely morally significant. From Skinner's example, it is not even clear if there really is a moral violation. With this example, Skinner leaves us unable to distinguish real guilt from a feeling merely mimicking it.

To explain the psychological experience of moral guilt, there needs to be a better example where there is a clear moral violation at stake. For example, suppose someone in a thrill-seeking mood casually murders some stranger, and then later becomes haunted by the experience. Surely this "being haunted" makes no sense if the stranger has the value of an insect. But given the moral significance of murdered person's value of life, the above Skinnarian interpretation—now with this example in mind—becomes ridiculously insufficient to explain the murderer's subsequent horror and self-contempt.

It is easy to identify this same reductionistic approach towards moral, metaphysical and religious truths with other mainline psychological thinkers. For example, with Freud, religion is explained in terms of neurosis, conscience in terms of superego, value and morality in terms of sublimation, freedom in terms of determinism, and the realm of the spiritual merely in terms of matter. Instead of the possibility of persons being authentically motivated by transcendent[46] values and truth, motivation for both Skinner and Freud is now explained immanently in terms of instincts, needs and conditioning. The problem is not a debate about whether certain psychological structures exist, such as the superego or sublimation, as these structures can co-exist with morality, but about whether they can alone sufficiently explain morality without reductionism.

Notice that this focus on the empirical nature of psychology not only restricts the realm that psychology studies, but it also focuses exclusively on the lower spheres of motivation. If students are habitually at the mercy of the scientific "experts" (first criticism), they will typically also fail to notice this reductionistic approach (second criticism), despite the fact that it will often contradict their own lived experience and common sense.

Third, the assertion that *all* psychological phenomena are empirical or scientific in nature is not even itself a scientific assertion because empirical science neither deals with absolute assertions nor with insights into the universal natures (or essences) of things.

What scientific observation or set of observations could ever yield this claimed "insight" that *all* of psychology is empirical? No empirical observation or set of observations could ever justify such a claim. To really justify it, one would have to mean that "it belongs to the *inner nature* (or essence) of all the objects that psychology studies that they are empirical," similar to the claim that it belongs to the inner nature of all instances of, say, responsibility to presuppose freedom. Knowledge of essences goes beyond inductively totaling up individual empirical instances because there is always the possibility of exceptions. With a science of empirical phenomena, it is important to steer away from absolute claims. To go back to an earlier example, the fact that one or 50 or 50,000 swans observed in Europe are white obviously does not prove that *all* swans are white, especially since some Australian swans are in fact black.

In contrast, I do not know from a sampling of observable cases that *responsibility presupposes freedom* or that *2+2=4*—I know it even from one case—and I rather know these things in principle and therefore in all possible cases. The basis for my certainty that *responsibility presupposes freedom* is not merely that I have never encountered an instance of responsibility without freedom; it is rather that I (positively) "see" into the inner essence structure of responsibility via intellectual intuition that it must presuppose freedom. This is similar to my seeing the strict impossibility of something both existing and not-existing simultaneously (in exactly the same sense and time) or of 2+2 equaling 5. These insights measure empirical observations, not the reverse. The discipline that studies the nature of things is philosophy, not empirical science.

In contrast to this kind of intellectual seeing, with sensible objects, what is given are empirical intuitions into really existing, individual instances of some phenomena and not any insight into their universal natures. Seeing an individual swan does not give us any intuition into its respective general essence (into "swan-ness"). Any species understanding of swans is only given inductively by inferring its general nature (species) from observations of really existing particular swans. But with philosophical (and mathematical) objects, there is the possibility of an insight into the universal itself, even from one instance. I can intellectually "see" into the universal essence structure of responsibility that it must presuppose freedom.[47]

If a person has an insight into the (universal) nature of something, an absolute claim makes sense. But empirical science does not work with universal essence structures. It rather only works by way of observation into really existing, sensible particulars and inductive generalizations (Chapter 6) from them, which is why the conclusions of science are never absolute.

Finally, fourth, I want to develop here the idea that we only know of the conscious subject performing psychic acts through our everyday lived experience and not, strictly speaking, via any empirical observation, which only observes sensible phenomena "from without." It is granted that things given empirically are also given in experience (insofar as both naïve lived experience and specialized scientific observation are in principle experiential). That does not mean that everything given in our lived experience is therefore empirical. For, after all, both intrinsic value and our own inner conscious experience are also given to us in our lived experience, but they are not empirical.

Consider how our inner conscious life can be contrasted with empirical experience. Empirical phenomena are only given on the "outside" of our conscious life, as sensible objects given over against our conscious self. In contrast, our conscious, personal self and the acts performed by the self are given on the "inside"* of our conscious life[48] and are clearly not sensibly given. Both of these kinds of experiences are constitutive of our lived experience of reality. Yet, empirical objects are exclusively given only on the "outside," and empiricism at most only implicitly presupposes this "inside" experience while explicitly and exclusively affirming only "outer" empirical experience.

*INNER AND OUTER: CONSCIOUS LIFE AND BEHAVIOR

The identification of *experience* with *empirical experience* stems from modern psychology's quest to be a natural (or empirical) science, whose exclusive method is the empirical method. This, however, leads to the problem of how to deal with inner experience.

This is not a problem for the pure, natural sciences (biology, chemistry, physics) because they do not actually study the content of conscious acts, but at most only the causes, conditions and effects of them. Their object of study, therefore, is already "outer." This is, however, a problem with psychological behaviorism because psychology has to center (at least implicitly) around the phenomenon of consciousness, and yet conscious life is private and "inner," while behaviour is public and "outer."

One "solution" of this problem goes back to the behaviorist, John Watson (1878-1958), who identifies the "soul" with having an inner conscious life (Chapter 5), and then simply denies the existence of the soul as non-scientific nonsense. He, in this way, repudiates what is the clearest and most obvious of realities: conscious life.

A second, more reasonable—although also inadequate—solution is the one taken by much of contemporary psychology, which is to implicitly presuppose consciousness with as little direct theoretical attention to it as possible, while at the same time applying the empirical method to behavior. The problem with this solution is that a crucial dimension of psychology—inner conscious life—is ignored.

A third solution is given by the psychology textbook writer Dennis Goon, who distinguishes between "overt" and "covert behaviors,"[49] with inner conscious life described as "covert behavior." By this reasoning, psychology can have its cake and eat it too! That is, talk only about behavior while retaining inner conscious states.

One wonders, however, how this solution squares with Goon's further emphasis on the empirical method, as he does not even begin to explain how this method works with "covert behaviors." For, after all, dictionaries tell us that *behavior* is simply synonymous with *conduct* and *performance*, which are obviously observable. What possible sense then does a "covert conduct" or a "covert performance" make? His solution seems to be a mere "linguistic coverup" than any serious attempt to explain the relation and dependency of behavior with inner conscious states.

This distinction between "outside" and "inside" is evidence of a real difference of kind between the brain and the conscious self. For no matter how sophisticated the scientific instrumentation used, they will simply never "reach" the actual "inner" content of what a conscious subject thinks and wills and loves. Why? Because a conscious subject and psychic acts are psychic realities that are only grasped from within by the individual having the experience. Thus, they exist on another level of being and reality than anything that can be observed empirically—observed from without—such as with the brain.[50]

The above overall case for the non-empirical dimension of psychology may, for the sake of the argument, seem persuasive. But, if true, how do you explain this massive assent to the claim that psychology in fact is an empirical science? One does find this claim without qualification throughout all of contemporary psychology, by its mainline introductory textbooks, by *The American Psychological Association*, and by most of its major thinkers. Why is it that no one mentions any other alternative, such as the inwardness of personal experience or the understanding of essence structures (for the understanding of motivation and the nature of the person)?

In response to this question, I want to conclude this chapter by presenting a theory as to why contemporary psychology has come to this point.

Imagine yourself as an author of some academic article or text, in whatever field. You will have a choice: on any particular issue, you can either go with the prevailing cultural understanding (whether of the wider society or the academic culture) or go against it. If you decide to go with the culture, you will typically not bother with trying to find reasons and arguments supporting your position. No one, after all, will be debating it with you. But if you decide to go against the basic cultural understanding, you had better be prepared to explain and defend it. The one thing you cannot do is go against the culture without some explanation and defense because no one will publish, much less read, your writing.

This above explanation, of course, still begs the question of what explains the presence of this "basic acceptance" of empiric*ism* in our own culture, if it is so false? How did we as a culture get here? Specifically, I would like to give an account explaining our own intellectual, cultural context[51] for why it is that mainline psychology senses no need to justify what is to my mind not only not obviously[52] or self-evidently true, it (psychological empiric*ism*) is not even true at all.

When philosophy professors teach history of philosophy, they notice—especially in Renaissance (roughly sixteenth and seventeenth centuries) and Modern (eighteenth and nineteenth centuries) philosophy—that different significant philosophers tend towards one of two "poles." They either tend towards rationalism (as if *all* questions can be settled by purely philosophical and mathematical investigation) or empiricism (as if everything ultimately goes back to sense perception), or some combination of the two positions. It is interesting to note how this tension has historically played itself out in our culture, especially in the light of the explosion of knowledge within the natural or empirical sciences during that time. Our culture has obviously been greatly impacted by the success of these sciences, not only practically and technologically transforming our lives, but also by the way we (theoretically and philosophically) think as well.

It is worthwhile sketching out how the empirical sciences have affected philosophy, and then in turn how philosophy and the sciences both affect culture. At first, philosophers will notice how science will sometimes overturn in a convincing fashion venerable philosophical/pre-scientific speculation[53] about the natural world held for centuries, such as, for instance, the teaching concerning the earth being the unmoved center of the solar system. Such ideas will not remain in purely scientific circles for long, as they eventually seep into the cultural understanding of the natural world. And philosophers will surely notice how revolutionary the natural sciences can be to the culture, both theoretically and practically (technologically), and so they will naturally begin to be "proactive" in their philosophical thinking by emphasizing more and more an empirically oriented philosophical approach. With the continued success of the empirical, natural sciences, this empirical, philosophical approach will, over time, become more dominant, culminating in the radical empiricism of David Hume (1711-1776). Even though Hume was an eighteenth-century philosopher, his influence has never been greater than today, insofar as his philosophy has not only influenced other philosophies, it has—together (of course) with the natural sciences—also in its turn decisively influenced the culture.

Although Hume was himself not a professor, his writings tremendously influenced the philosophical professoriate. At first, these more empirically-oriented philosophers and professors did not have much of an effect on the wider culture, as they generally influenced only their own students. But over time, students taught by them became teachers, and they, of course, influenced their own students, and on and on. Any foundational philosophical idea— whether true or false—if not stopped early, will tend over time to influence an entire culture.

Now consider this cultural, philosophical influence from the point of view of the content of some actual philosophy. In the classroom, philosophical argumentation is considered as a whole, including, of course, all its premises and conclusions. But, over a period of generations, as a particular philosophy tends to "seep" into the culture (as professors will teach other future teachers), the full arguments *as arguments* given in the classroom—again, whether true or false—will in the wider culture tend to degenerate and wither. What will eventually be left from within the culture will only be the conclusions, culturally transformed into mere assumptions (or even prejudices), as they will not even be identified as conclusions of arguments. They will become the new intellectual "prism"* through which the culture will then view reality.

*THE SIGNIFICANCE OF CULTURAL "PRISMS"

The influence of a culture on individuals should not be underestimated. It is very difficult to go against the trends (explicit and implicit assumptions) of one's own culture, leading to one example of what psychologists call "cognitive dissonance," in which a person might think one way but the culture as a whole thinks the opposite. It is obviously far less stressful simply to accept the cultural norms "to get along." Such a tactic typically works unless the culture itself becomes deeply crazy, such as Nazi Germany in the mid-1930s.

On the other hand, it is also important not to overestimate the influence of a culture, as if all our opinions are reducible to mere individual expressions of cultural ones, which leads to the conclusion of a cultural determinism whereby we cannot think for ourselves. No, we all need to "grow a spine," so to speak, and continually strive to think for ourselves, despite periodic cognitive dissonance with some significant other or the culture at large.

One crucial way of "thinking for oneself" is to explicitly and even-handedly consider the evidence for positions, especially concerning psychological evidence that dovetails with philosophy. Thinking about the degree and kind (whether empirical, moral, metaphysical, ethical, the word of others, etc.) of evidence is a good habit to develop, as opposed to merely assuming some position because it is stated in some text or supposed by one's own culture.

In psychology, there exists undeniable pressure to consider itself a "hard" science, that is, rigorous in methods and approach, without which you are merely in a sea of unsubstantiated theory. Of course, the empirical approach is appropriate to those objects that are suited to its method. But this pressure becomes itself a prejudice if one tries to apply it to objects not suited to that method.

So, applied to our present-day cultural appropriation of empiricism, what began as a philosophical debate between rationalism and empiricism ends— at least in our society—with empiricism being merely a given, as being "obviously" true. But this "obviousness" does not go back to simple truths grasped by the common sense person (Chapter 1) or to some empirical, scientific observation or even set of observations. It rather goes back only to a pseudo-obviousness of cultural presuppositions merely assumed to be true, given the success of scientific progress over the past centuries. This is precisely the situation we now face, not only in our society in general but also specifically in contemporary psychology, considering itself (obviously!) to be an empirical science.

This is another reason why thinking philosophically about one's discipline is so important: cultural prisms exist which may or may not be true. Either way, they need to be looked at and investigated, not merely assuming their truth. Are they really true as we assume them to be? They might be true or false. Either way, let us stop merely assuming their truth and look for the evidence.

Notice that all the above criticism against empiricism can be eliminated by one simple move: instead of saying that *all* psychology (or *all* knowledge) is empirical, why not just say that *many*—as opposed to *all*—problems in psychology can be explained empirically? Then there needs to be further investigation into what constitutes these other methods and means of investigation. It was already admitted that many aspects of psychology can only be explained empirically, such as with many aspects of learning theory, abnormal and developmental psychology, and so forth. Nothing asserted above opposes that approach.

Now let us imagine someone disagreeing with my claim that the discipline of psychology is too narrowly conceived, holding instead that all psychology really is completely empirical in nature. All right, now consider justifying this position without either pretending that it is self-evident or with thinking that this question can be determined empirically without merely presupposing what needs to be proved. Argue for it with evidence (and take note when psychology textbooks do not give that evidence). Show how that assertion is true, and then notice just how philosophical your resulting argument will be.

Chapter 4

The Subject Matter of Psychology (Part A): The Conscious Personal Self

What does the science of psychology study? The answer to this question seems obvious…until you actually try to answer it. Most objects of philosophical investigation are like that, both seemingly easy and yet strangely difficult to answer.* They are "easy" because all philosophical objects go back to and are grounded in our lived experience.

*SELF-EVIDENCE DOES NOT MEAN *EASY TO SEE*

For example, consider the philosophical insight that *responsibility presupposes freedom*. The truth of this insight is in principle accessible to everyone, and of course, it is easy to see. Other insights, however, can only be seen on the basis of thought and effort. For example, the principle of non-contradiction (that *contradictory opposite assertions cannot both be true*) is fairly easy to see, although not quite as easy as the first example. But the principle of excluded middle—that *contradictory opposite assertions cannot both be false*—is more difficult to see and justify.

The truth of all three of these principles are in principle self-evident (in the sense that the truth of these assertions is not mediated by other states of affairs [Chapter 6]) and public, but without implying that they are all necessarily easy to see, or equally easy to see. Nor do they imply that everyone in fact sees them.

Since the objects that philosophy studies go back to no new or different source of experience other than our common lived experience, everyone has at least an implicit sense for them. And yet, as Augustine noted long ago with his own example of time, how do you explain what time is?[54] Of course, everyone has a sense of this reality. On the other hand, it is very difficult to explain theoretically. There are unsuspected depths, difficult to penetrate and understand. The same thing goes with person, psychic acts, freedom, self-presence, truth, morality, and God, all of which philosophy tries to penetrate and, to some extent, understand. This helps explain why it is that philosophy is often so difficult to read, despite its link to common sense and our common lived experience.*

*ANOTHER REASON FOR THE DIFFICULTY OF PHILOSOPHY

Besides the aspect of "hidden depths" to philosophical objects of study, there is also the problem of how many times philosophers have to go beyond both what is self-evidently given in experience. Not every insight has the clarity of *responsibility presupposes freedom*, which the common sense person also sees. There are also issues that go beyond strict, logical inferences from self-evident insights. Often philosophers do not see a phenomenon clearly—because of its difficulty—and so they will say (or, at least hopefully say...as opposed to giving the impression of seeing what they do not in fact see) something like this: *since this phenomenon is not so clearly given to me, this is how I think it might be. This is what makes the best sense to me, giving us the most complete account with the simplest explanation.*

This kind of explanation—giving the most complete account with the simplest explanation—is also found in natural science. For example, all of us now think that the sun is the center of the solar system. Our culture thinks this because we have been told so by reputable scientists. Why do they think it? It is not from any sensible, empirical observation, which given the vast distances involved, make any such observation impossible even by the most sophisticated scientific instruments. It is rather because the mathematics explaining and predicting the movements of the planets in a heliocentric way are conceptually simpler than the older, Ptolemaic understanding, which places the earth at the center of the solar system. Here we have an application of what is known as Occam's Razor—explaining more and in a simpler way—to justify this move from the Ptolemaic to the Copernican understanding of the universe.

This more speculative, theoretical approach of Occam's Razor is one application of what is more generally called "inference to best explanation." Thus, what justifies the Copernican approach in the above example as the "best inference," given the evidence. Both principles (inference to the best explanation and Occam's Razor) are used extensively in philosophy as well as the empirical sciences, insofar as their interpretations go beyond what is intuitively and deductively given.

What is the object of psychology? This is a basic philosophical question, delimiting possible objects or subject matter for the beginning of a scientific investigation cannot itself be a product of that science itself, insofar as that science does not yet exist, and philosophy is especially about both the beginnings (and ends or purposes) of things. So, what is the ground zero object of psychological investigation? What are the objects that psychology studies?

I submit that the center-point of psychology is this: *The discipline of psychology studies that dimension of human nature that is either conscious or oriented towards conscious life, as well as the causes and conditions for consciousness* (Chapter 5). Thus, for instance, for a wish or a thought to be actualised each must necessarily be conscious. But if not actualized, they can still somehow exist as latent, either in memory or as somehow unconsciously repressed. And even if they are unconscious, one can say these psychic acts are—as psychological realities—still oriented towards consciousness and thus are proper objects of psychological investigation.

In Chapter 2, progress was made to identify psychic acts—such as with willing, loving, hating, deducing, promising, etc.—as one kind of object of psychological investigation, insofar as they are themselves conscious realities. They are not only oriented to consciousness but also are, while being performed, essentially conscious.* They are thus not derivative in merely being products of psychic acts (such as a promise is a product of an act of promising and a thought is from an act of thinking) nor dependent upon psychic acts as their "fruit" (such as the experience of pleasure, happiness and despair that can follow from them).

*CONSCIOUSNESS AND REPRESSION

The psychiatrist, Karen Horney (1885-1952), has an interesting observation about the connection between these repressed psychic contents and consciousness when she states,

> [W]e cannot fool ourselves … [W]e observe ourselves better than we are aware of doing, just as we usually observe others better than we are aware of doing—as shown, for example, in the correctness of the first impression we get from a person—but we may have stringent reasons for not taking cognizance of our observations. For the sake of saving repetitive explanations, I shall use the term 'register' when I mean that we know what is going on within us without our being aware of it.[55]

What Horney claims is that even with something being unconscious via repression, there remains some residue from that repressed content that still remains within actual consciousness, not merely oriented to consciousness but as somehow implicit, albeit fractured, disguised and misinterpreted within our present conscious life. Thus, repressed contents are for Horney never quite gone, and there always remains some conscious link to them. Thus, a repressive personality is one who has to be continually repressing the very same content, insofar as an ever-increasing awareness is continually "bubbling up," trying to break through from implicit to a more explicit and threatening conscious awareness. This theory would then explain why a repressed person is continually emotionally exhausted and why the content repressed can sometimes be exposed and brought to explicit consciousness—insofar as it is never completely gone in the first place—perhaps with professional psychological assistance.

Psychic acts, however, are not yet the epicenter of all psychological investigation because these acts are always performed by a conscious subject. They only exist "at the mercy of" conscious subjects bringing them into being. Thus, the conscious subject is (metaphysically) the more fundamental reality, as opposed to the conscious acts themselves. The personal self is the center of all psychological phenomena. And since we are not angels (that is, pure spirits), this "personal self" is in an intimate unity with its physical body to form our human nature: body and soul.*

*THE RELATION BETWEEN *PERSONAL SELF* AND *SOUL*

In this text, I am using the term *soul* in its standard philosophical sense—going back to Aristotle (383-320 BC)—to refer to a life principle animating a body. There are, of course, different kinds of souls or life principles, as there are differing kinds of living beings. For instance, what differentiates a vegetable life principle (or soul) from an animal soul are the different kinds of powers a living being possesses. If a living being possesses sense perception, it is an animal. If a living, bodily being possesses not only the powers of sense perception, but also distinctly personal powers—of intellect and will—it possesses a personal soul.

In this text, I will tend to use the term *personal self* more than *soul*, not because the *soul* is somehow illegitimate but merely because the *personal self* is a more modern term.

I want to begin this analysis of the personal self by being as experiential and psychological as possible. One way of doing this is to consider the following experiences: "*I* am now thinking...or...*I* am now willing...or...*I* am now loving...or...despairing or promising or commanding, etc." Notice that with all these instances of psychic acts, all of us implicitly make a distinction without hardly noticing it: between the psychic acts and the conscious self who performs them. In other words, no one ever says, "thinking has taken place. Gee, I wonder whose act it is?" No, the experience is always, "*I* think." The "I" is given in the experience. Why? Because we are always consciously present to ourselves as the ones performing psychic acts. Notice that I am here making an experiential, not merely theoretical or inferential point: our very self is given in the performance of our own psychic acts.

Perhaps one reason why this may still seem strange is that when someone thinks of consciousness, he or she is usually thinking more about the objects experienced than the self who performs and experiences them. So, for example, if I am intently focused on perceiving, say, a mountain, it seems reasonable to assume that my consciousness is completely swallowed up by its object: the mountain. Actually, however, there are two dimensions of personal consciousness, in the sense of being one reality (consciousness) having two poles, like the earth being one entity having a north and south pole. Despite their distinction, each dimension presupposes the other to form one unified conscious experience. These two poles are intentional (or frontal) consciousness and (lateral) self-presence.* The central focus here concerns self-presence, insofar as it is ground zero for our conscious life and therefore for the discipline of psychology. However, I want here to begin with intentional[56] consciousness because it is easier to explain.

*FRONTAL AND LATERAL POLES OF CONSCIOUS LIFE

Both terms—*frontal* and *lateral*—are spatial metaphors referring to the two kinds of conscious experience (intentional, conscious acts and self-presence), which are both in their own nature non-material phenomena. As will be explained below, intentional consciousness refers to those acts and responses that have an object referent. These are acts and responses that are essentially about something, given *in front of us*, as over-against our inner conscious experience. Whereas self-presence refers to that experience of ourselves that is experienced not frontally, but coming inward laterally or *from the side*.

As a technical, philosophical term, the term *intentional* has a different, wider meaning than its usual English usage. In normal English, this term means "done on purpose." In its philosophical sense (the sense used in this text), it means "consciousness of an object." Naturally, something "done on purpose" is one example of an intentional act in this wider, technical meaning. But loving, promising, self-reflection, perceiving, hating, judging, commanding, deducing, knowing, and so forth are also (in this second, wider meaning) intentional as well. Also, while this phenomenon of intentionality typically refers to the external world, there are exceptions. Illusions and the experience of self-reflection are intentional as well—insofar as they are "about something"—and yet they are not "out there" in the external world, as they are only creations or reflections of a conscious being.

The two poles of our conscious life are intentionality and self-presence. The first pole refers to intentional conscious experiences, which are essentially "about something." All intentional psychic acts involve a consciousness of an object. Sense perception is intentional in that sense: whether of seeing or touching or hearing other persons, trees, mountains, etc. I do not just see or hear; I see or hear some object, such as a person. There are also purely immaterial objects, such as the nature of justice or happiness or when someone reflects back and objectifies their own act of willing or thinking, which is self-reflection. I cannot have a perceptual experience without some object perceived. Thus, experience and object are, with this act—as well as with all the other intentional conscious experiences—essentially united, insofar as I cannot perform these acts without the corresponding consciousness of its respective object. For example, I cannot simply grieve. I have to grieve "over something," such as the death of some loved one. I do not just will; I will something. I do not just love; I love someone. Both willing and loving are essentially "about something."

The second pole of conscious experience is lateral self-presence, which is intimately united to intentional experiences and yet distinct from them. This kind of experience goes in a different direction—inward rather than outward—not only away from all external objects, but away from all objects whatsoever. This dimension of consciousness refers to my awareness of myself in the act of performing other, intentional acts. But it is an awareness of myself as a subject performing conscious acts, not as an object of thought. For example, whereas I encounter myself via self-reflection as an object, with self-presence I am aware of myself as a subject performing intentional, conscious acts, including the act of self-reflection. I am present to myself (subjectively) as the one performing all my own intentional conscious acts, forming the subjective pole of all my own intentional, psychic acts.

Consider as a second example self-presence within the context of the intentional experience of grieving. Grief is essentially "about something," let us say, the death of some beloved person. Notice how a person while grieving can be completely engrossed over its intentional object—such as this death of a loved one—and so not be thinking about anything else, including herself at all. And yet, even when so engrossed, she is surely aware that she is the one grieving, even though she is not at all thinking of herself as an object at all.

Let us say this grieving person suddenly becomes aware of someone else observing her crying and becomes self-conscious and embarrassed. Notice how this self-awareness of herself—now as a self-reflective object of thought—will have the effect of at least temporarily cutting her off from the source of her grief, which is her consciousness of the death of the loved one. This new self-consciousness (of herself as an object) will now make it more difficult for her to grieve, as she is now distracted from the object and source of her grief.

Here one can see with the intentional response of grief how it is that the object and the response (or act) form a unified experience. There is no separating the object from the experience without destroying the response. For you cannot grieve without an object motivating it. Without the object, the response of grief becomes unintelligible. It is the same for all the other intentional acts and responses: a unity of object and response.

One can also discover a kind of unity within self-presence: a unity of consciousness and real being. For the being that is present is the really existing self. Thus, the person who is conscious of herself as the one grieving is…herself! With lateral self-presence, we encounter not a mere idea or intentional object, but the reality of the self.

Consider now the psychological significance of both self-reflection and self-presence.

First, it is through self-presence that we get not only really existing being—the being of the self—but also a certain knowledge of this reality. This certainty is different from knowledge of objects given intentionally. For notice how these objects, at least in principle, can be subjectivized away. Someone could always say: *that thing you think you are perceiving* (intentionally) *is actually only dreamt.* And, I must admit, there have been times when I really have been fooled in this way.

In contrast, this way of debunking (or discrediting)—by claiming that the experience is illusory—cannot be accomplished with self-presence. For if someone tries to subjectivize that lateral awareness away and say, *you were only dreaming!* I can respond and say, *okay. But even if that is true, notice that only a really existing being can dream!* Thus, while it is possible to subjectivize intentional objects away, it is not possible with lateral self-presence. I have here with the reality of the self, given laterally, a special kind of epistemological certainty of my own real existence.

The reason for bringing this up is because there are many thinkers who deny the very existence of the self. For instance, the philosopher David Hume (1711-

1776) states, "For my part, when I enter most intimately into what I call *myself*, I always stumble on some particular perception or other, of heat or cold, light or shade, love or hatred, pain or pleasure. I never catch *myself* at any time without a perception, and never can observe anything but the perception" [emphasis in original].[57] It seems that Hume is looking for the self as if it were an (intentional) object of perception instead of the being who is conscious. Since he cannot find the self as an object of perception, he thinks that the self (or soul) is merely an illegitimate fictional holdover from religion.

Another example comes from B. F. Skinner, who treats the self as merely a made-up idea, as he states, "It may seem inconsistent to ask the reader to 'keep a point in mind' when he has been told that mind is an *explanatory fiction...*" [emphasis added].[58]

Freud treats it as a term which refers to a conscious manifestation of a more primary biological reality.* He states, "Being conscious is in the first place a purely descriptive **term**, resting on perception of the most immediate and certain character" [emphasis in text].[59]

*ONE PSYCHOLOGY TEXTBOOK EXPLANATION OF THE CONSCIOUS SELF

Although Hume, Freud and Skinner are major thinkers in philosophy and psychology, you might be tempted to think their influence has perhaps waned in psychology. How often does your typical introductory psychology student come in contact with these interpretations? Yet, one might note how close the position of the well-known psychology textbook writer David Myers is to Freud's. He states, "You love, laugh, and cry with your body. Without your body—your genes, your brain, your appearance—you are, indeed, nobody."[60]

In this passage, he implies that the self is nothing but a conscious manifestation of an underlying, merely biological reality. This seems very close to, if not the same as, Freud's position. Myers is making what is to my mind metaphysically breath-taking claims. Whether they are true or false, they are coming from people who otherwise think that metaphysics is archaic and medieval.

The empiricism that these thinkers espouse makes it seem to them that the very reality of the self is questionable. However, once someone takes into account the experience of lateral self-presence, we have a way not only to establish the real existence of the self, but even a certain knowledge of this existence.

Second, notice the differing intensities of the subjective self-presence: some people only have a superficial (lateral) contact with themselves, and if so, they seem rather "vacant," like Prince Valium of the screwball comedy movie *Spaceballs.* But even he cannot completely escape his own self-presence to himself, insofar as someone who is conscious cannot completely escape their own self. In contrast, there are people like Karol Wojtyla (the late Pope John Paul II), who famously had the ability to give himself completely to everyone in his company.

These differing intensities of self-presence are actually an excellent criterion for the depth of a personality. The stronger the self-presence, the more persons are able to enter into situations and give themselves to others.[61] This strength of self-presence is, of course, utterly different from continuous and immature self-absorption, as (non-intentional or lateral) self-presence is distinct from (intentional or frontal) self-reflection. It seems obvious that reflection should be given to that which can lead to the strengthening of the power of self-presence, especially for counselors and the counseling profession, who need to work on *being present* to those they are counseling. In fact, awareness of and growth in self-presence is central for everyone because we are all in relationships with others. This is one criterion of love: the ability to give ourselves to another by being present to that other.

Third, concerning self-reflection, reflecting back upon one's self is an excellent thing to do...periodically. For if persons never reflect back upon themselves, one could rightly say of such persons that they really do not know themselves, insofar as knowledge is essentially intentional, or "about something."[62] On the other hand, if someone is constantly reflecting back on his or herself, one wonders just how narcissistic—or at least how immature—that person is. Part of growing up as a person entails the realization that I am not always the "theme" (that is, the central focus) of every situation. There is something to be said about "noble self-forgetfulness," of being present to something or someone other than yourself, and especially to those things possessing high intrinsic value. But of course, this self-forgetfulness only applies to forsaking any *constant* (intentional) pre-occupation with one's self, not with any attempt to get rid of one's own (non-intentional) self-presence or occasional self-reflection.

If the personal self really exists, what kind of real existence does it have? Is the self substantially* distinct from and yet united to the body forming the whole human being: body and soul? Or, alternatively, can conscious life be completely explained in terms of the body, say, as a property of the brain? Is the notion of substance important for psychology? If so, how?

*WHAT IS A SUBSTANCE?

A substance is a philosophical/metaphysical term referring to that dimension of a really existing being that "stands-in-itself" and is not a part or property of something else. Sometimes you can find two substantially distinct beings that nonetheless enter into a unity. One finds this in a marriage between two persons becoming united "in one flesh," and it can be found (analogously) in the unity of body and soul that constitutes one human person.

In contrast, a living organ, such as a heart or liver, is not substantially distinct from the body because it is obviously a *part* of the body. These living parts cannot stand on their own, at least as independent, living entities. Also, the *properties* of a material thing being gaseous or rectangular, etc., do not stand-in-themselves as they are grounded in the substance that bears them. Neither parts nor properties are substantial in nature.

A substance, in contrast to parts and properties, refers to that dimension of a being that can "stand in itself" and is not grounded in anything else; it is rather is an "endpoint-in-being." Thus, for example, a barbell could weigh 5 or 10 pounds, as this weight is grounded in the substantial reality of the barbell. But the substance of the barbell itself is not grounded in anything else. It is rather an endpoint in being.

If the soul is substantially distinct from the body, it follows that the soul could in principle survive the death of the body. In contrast, if the soul or conscious self is merely a property of the body, such as being somehow the particular way the brain is organized, then when the brain dies, the soul would die as well.

On the other hand, it is also clear how the soul is dependent on the body. This dependency is found in countless ways: the proper functioning of our brain physiology, bio-chemistry, even our brain temperature are empirically necessary conditions for the possibility of our conscious life. Our souls, our personal self, may survive the death of our bodies, and if so, are substantial in nature. But they are also clearly incomplete substances, insofar as they are ordered to and empirically dependent upon the body.

I think reflecting upon whether the personal self is substantially distinct from the body is actually crucial for psychology. The reason is this: because the substantial reality of the soul (or personal self) is tied to the reality of freedom. Our personal life stands or falls by whether personal beings are free (Chapter 9), and freedom requires something more than the soul being merely a property of the body.

I will begin by making two arguments for the actual substantial reality of the soul. Even though the notion of substance seems unscientific* and antiquated, I think that when it comes to persons, we cannot simply jettison this notion. The first argument will first make the case for the immateriality of the soul so as to distinguish it from the body. And then the second argument will make the case that if the soul is free, it has to have a certain kind of independence from the body.

*WHY THE NOTION OF SUBSTANCE IS NOT IMPORTANT FOR SCIENCE?

In this box, I want to explain the rationale for why the notion of substance has fallen out of science, and then in the following text, make an argument for why this notion needs to be rehabilitated for psychology.

The notion of *substance* is not important for natural science because, like *value*, both ideas refer to non-empirical dimensions of really existing beings. These dimensions are rationally understood by our mind instead of being empirically intuited.

One contemporary philosophical historian, William Lawhead, points out one important historical, scientific root of this non-scientific character of substance. He quotes Sir Isaac Newton (1643-1727), who states,

> Hitherto I have not been able to discover the cause of those properties of gravity from phenomena, and I frame no hypotheses; for whatever is not deduced from the phenomena is to be called a hypothesis; and hypotheses, whether metaphysical or physical, whether of occult qualities or mechanical, have no place in experimental science.[63]

Then Lawhead comments upon this passage as follows,

> This represents a significant turning point in the history of thought, for Newton was telling scientists to give up all attempts to deal with essences and the underlying reality of things [such

as the notion of substance]. Henceforth, science is to only describe the patterns of empirical phenomena. The reality that lies behind, underneath, or beyond the phenomena cannot be scientifically comprehended.[64]

One can grant that it is not the business of empirical science to investigate values, universal natures and the "underlying reality of things" (that is, substance). That does not mean these dimensions of reality, including non-empirical psychological realities, do not, therefore, exist unless one first assumes that a scientific approach exhausts all the dimensions of reality, which is the thesis of empiric*ism*. A purely scientific approach to reality does not even exhaust our naïve experience of reality, whereby we intuitively—albeit typically implicitly—grasp the substantial reality of mountains, cars and persons.

So why discuss the notion of substance? It is granted that this idea is not crucial for the scientific understanding the physics of material things, which was Newton's focus. My point is that without at least an implicit awareness of substance, one not only does violence to common sense and our naïve lived experience of reality—insofar as nobody actually experiences the things of the world as mere de-substantialized shadows—but also fails to do justice to the uniquely personal dimension of conscious being, especially of our freedom and thus of our human nature.

The first evidence for the immaterial reality of the soul goes back to lateral self-presence, noticed long ago by Augustine (354-430). He saw that everything material is psychically given as objects of our conscious life. This means that awareness of material reality is always given to us intentionally, as objects of our perception or reflection. Specifically, the brain—despite its close relation to conscious activities—is also only given to us as an object of consciousness. It is never laterally experienced. In contrast, our inner conscious life—given to us laterally and non-intentionally—betrays no trace of anything material. What is given to us laterally are our own psychic acts of loving, willing, promising, and so forth, as well as our conscious self, and these are all immaterial realities. Thus, in our inmost contact with our own conscious selves via lateral self-presence, where there is a coinciding—an identity—between consciousness and being where nothing material is given, as everything material is given only intentionally.[65]

Secondly, consider freedom. If freedom is not a mere illusion and persons really do possess this power, then the idea of the personal self being reduced to a mere property of the body—such the personal self being reducible to some particular set of neural pathways—becomes absurd because neural pathways are themselves merely the effects of caused products of genetics and environmental experiences. Certainly, these pathways can themselves be causal, but only in the sense of links in a causal chain of "caused causes" or secondary causes. Freedom, in contrast, refers to just the contradictory opposite of *caused* states, to the initiation of acts or actions that are *not-caused*. What this suggests—again, assuming the reality of freedom—is that the being of the self is not only distinct, it is even substantially distinct from the body. In contrast, nobody thinks that the brain, much less biochemical events inside the brain, are substantially distinct from the body. They simply follow the trends of the body.

Why does freedom imply substantiality? One way of characterizing authentic substances is to say that they are "centered-in-themselves." Neither a property nor a part of something else is "centered in itself," as they are centered in the substance that bears it. The brain is clearly given as a part of its body. Therefore, its "center" lies outside itself and with the body considered as a whole. This is why the brain, much less brain processes, cannot act "in their own name," as they are merely processes determined by the substance that bears it. However, if the personal self is free, it cannot be centered in anything, not itself if it is capable of acting as a first cause. In other words, if the personal self is free, it can act "in its own name," so to speak. If it were centered outside of itself, like a *mere* slave—if such a being exists[66]—in relation to his master, then the center of his being would lie outside of himself, in the will of the master. Just as I can think for myself, so can I also will in my own name. In fact, if the personal self were merely a slave of its body, continuously giving in to its own instincts and bodily desires, one would rightly say that this person's life is psychologically disordered. Disorder would then be the norm,* which is contradictory. Therefore, the conscious, personal self is substantially distinct not only from its body—insofar as it is not or at least should not acquiesce to become a mere slave of its body—but also from all other social institutions that may think of individual or groups of persons as mere cogs or slaves.

*DISTINGUISHING TWO SENSES OF "NORM"

There are two senses of the term *norm*. It can refer to a statistical average, or it can mean the appropriate, best or ideal measure of something. I am in the text using the term in its second sense. Even if most people will at times give away their birthright and let other people do their thinking and willing for them (which may be a statistical average state of mind for many people)—thus not acting as persons— the fact remains that they are persons, who possess the power to act freely and therefore should (ideally) exercise that power.

Naturally, one could respond to all this by claiming that human beings are not free, and if this claim is true, then the above argument collapses. Then the soul would simply follow the (instinctual) trends of its body, which is voluntary insofar as it is determined from within (Chapter 7). Exclusively following one's own instincts would then not be disordered but would be the most natural thing in the world, and all desiring could rightly be interpreted as simply a psychic extension of the processes of the body, hardly being "centered-in-itself."

If it is true that the essence (or nature) of what it means to be a person is to possess the powers of intellect and will, then an attack upon either (or both) powers is in effect an attack on the claim that human beings are persons. Maybe someone thinking this way will still use the term "person" to identify human beings, but its deeper meaning will be lost, and this person will really consider human beings as nothing but higher-order animals.

Whether the powers of intellect and will even exist—that is, whether human *persons* exist—is not only within the purview of psychology; it is one of the most foundational questions psychology can ask. Up to this point, however, the real existence of freedom was only presupposed—going back at least to common sense—which then became my central reason for claiming both the personal nature of human beings as well as of the personal self as being substantially distinct from the body that is united with it. But common sense can at times be wrong, and there are central characters in psychology who are famous determinists. This is why I must later return to the question of whether human beings actually possess this power of freedom (Chapter 9).

The theme of this chapter especially concerns lateral self-presence, which is at the basis of a person's conscious life. It is an important segway to the real existence and reality of the personal self, ground zero of our psychological life. Everything else about a person's psychological life will extend like spokes from the hub of the conscious, personal self. I want to now turn to some of these spokes.

Chapter 5

The Subject Matter of Psychology (Part B): Differing Kinds of Psychic Phenomena

The last chapter concerned the metaphysical epicenter of psychological reality: the embodied, personal self. Here we encounter not merely consciousness, but conscious being, where there is an identity between consciousness and being. And the kind of real being the self possesses is substantial in nature. Everything in psychology revolves around this center, with the personal self being the "hub" centering all the other "spokes" of further psychological objects of investigation.

Now I want to investigate some of these spokes going out, so to speak, from the personal self. My aim is obviously not to be exhaustive, as psychological textbooks will have far more detailed analyses of these and other spokes that obviously will go far beyond a philosophical approach. Rather, I want to identify those "spokes" apparent from a broader philosophical perspective. The effect will be to re-populate the psychological world along some familiar lines within contemporary psychology. This will be accomplished, of course, only in a formal or structural way, without the important complexity and wealth of content found in psychological textbooks.

Before beginning, there are three important differences to keep in mind between this (formal) philosophical psychological approach and contemporary psychology.

First, while space needs to be given to the rightful place of the empirical method within psychology, there will be no pretense that an exclusive application of a philosophical—or for that matter, an empirical—approach will explain all psychological phenomena.

Second, the different spokes will be measured against the central, unifying idea of psychology, which is consciousness. What connection do these different spokes have to conscious life? Some will be essentially conscious, others either the product or the "fruits" of conscious acts, and still others will be not conscious themselves but instead are merely the causes and conditions for conscious life. The further one goes out from this central idea of conscious life, the less central to psychology that datum becomes.

Third, there will be no shying away from making explicit metaphysical points and distinctions. The reason this point is important is because the kind of metaphysical reality a being possesses helps determine its significance for psychology. That which is metaphysically more real and central to the core of psychological reality, which is consciousness, will be of greater significance for psychology. For example, if the subject matter under consideration is the real (substantial) being of the conscious self, the very center of psychological reality is identified. If the subject matter concerns psychic acts performed by the conscious self or if the subject matter concerns expressive bodily behavior whereby someone can intuit (Chapter 6) conscious life, this remains close to that center.

If an object possesses the psychic reality of a mere appearance* (such as something being consciously experienced as big or small, pleasant or unpleasant), or possesses merely the kind of being of an illusion, such as a mere object of a dream, one is still dealing with essentially conscious phenomena that are of interest to psychology. But this interest will be less because of the impoverished kind of being mere appearances and illusions possess.

*THE SUBJECTIVISM OF APPEARANCES AND ILLUSIONS: HOW APPEARANCES PRESUPPOSE THINGS-IN-THEMSELVES

Earlier (Chapter 2), the difference between an appearance (big and small, fast and slow, etc.) and a being that appears (mountains, cars, persons, etc.) was discussed.

In contrast to both things-in-themselves (which are completely objective realities) and appearances-of-things (which are partially objective and partially subjective phenomena), illusions are "through and through" subjective realities. These subjective contributions are merely "produced" by the mind. As such, illusions only live "at the mercy" of our thinking and dreaming. Yet, they present themselves to us in our experience as being fully real, that is, fully objective, which is why we are fooled by them.

It is worth mentioning that both appearances and (especially) illusions seem similar to the approach of idealism (Chapter 1), insofar as both involve a subjective contribution to the object of the experience. With both appearances and illusions, our thinking becomes the measure of reality and not the reverse, that is, with reality being the measure of our thinking.

However, while the phenomena of appearances and illusions involve a subjective contribution of some object, this contribution can occur within a general framework of realism. This is especially clear with appearances, as it is through an appearance that we get at a thing which is not an appearance, but a thing-in-itself. Thus, the reality of appearances presupposes a context of realism—that is, of things existing in themselves—as it hardly makes sense to speak of appearances. Also, as long as one does not assert that *all* our experience is ultimately illusory, a la the *Matrix* movies, then the phenomena of illusions can occur and do occur within the context of a realist framework.

Not everything has to have the being of an appearance or illusion. Conversely, not everything given in my experience has the being of fully objective realities either, as appearances and illusions exist as well. A thoroughgoing idealist will think that only appearances and illusions exist, and a naïve-realist will think that only things-in-themselves exist. In actuality, all these differing kinds of phenomena exist.

All four above distinctions—the personal self, psychic acts, appearances and illusions—are either directly conscious or oriented to conscious life (such as with repressed psychic experiences), and thus are by varying degrees of interest to psychology. Then, finally, if the psychological data concerns the various causes and conditions for conscious life—which are not themselves conscious realities—their importance for our conscious life is more indirect, and yet they remain significant because of their relevance for explaining conscious life.

All science has to start somewhere. For example, consider geometry: the first of Euclid's axioms is that *things which are equal to the same thing are also equal to one another*. Notice how this starting point is not some mere arbitrary assumption, insofar as that would undermine everything else that follows from it. It is rather a self-evident insight. It is a "first" principle because all of Euclidean geometry depends upon it. Because it is self-evidently true, Euclid does not give an argument for that position. It is an axiom or ultimate first principle, not a conclusion from some other proof that is more ultimate.

In psychology, as elsewhere, it is crucially important to remember that, as Aristotle noted long ago, small mistakes at the beginning can very well lead to big mistakes down the road.[67] Consider again the assertion that *psychology deals with experiences that are either conscious or are oriented toward consciousness, as well as the causes and conditions of conscious life*. This statement, I think, is a better beginning for psychology as opposed to the first principle that *psychology is an empirical science,** as it yields a far more exact and illuminating identification as to the actual objects of psychological study.

*FIRST PRINCIPLE OF MAINLINE PSYCHOLOGY TEXTS

In the text above, I interpreted the assertion that *psychology is exclusively an empirical science* as a kind of first principle. This is because it is ubiquitously asserted by all mainline introductory texts and because this assertion is treated as if it were self-evidently true, insofar as it is not supported by anything else (at least by introductory psychology texts). If, however, it is asserted but in fact not self-evident, it becomes a mere assumption. And if it is merely assumed to be true, it is supported and grounded by nothing. In my view, this assertion is not only not self-evident, it is not even true.

Notice also how this putative psychological first principle is also methodological in nature. It is not about the content or subject matter of psychology, but rather only about how psychology is to be investigated.

If this interpretation— the exclusivity of psychology being empirical science as a first principle—is correct, this methodological starting point violates the principle that the method needs to follow and be determined by the content instead of vice versa. As noted above (Chapter 2), a methodological starting point as a first principle makes no sense. In contrast, the assertion that psychology centers around conscious phenomena is about the subject matter of psychology

So, after looking at the conscious self in Chapter 4, this chapter will continue the investigation by considering eight further objects (among others) of psychological study that in various ways and degrees orbit the central idea of consciousness: psychic acts, products of psychic acts, patterns of thinking and feeling, character formation, social relations and behavior, bodily behavioral patterns, causes and conditions of psychic acts, and a psychology of learning. I now want to investigate each in turn.

1. Psychic acts

Conscious acts performed by the personal self do not stand on their own, as they have to be performed by a conscious subject. They are by their nature psychic in the sense of being essentially conscious (when being performed) or at least oriented towards consciousness (when passive in memory or repressed). Here two of the three main kinds of psychic acts will be discussed:

volitional and affective acts. A third kind of psychic act, intellectual acts, will be investigated in Chapter 8, and volitional acts will be further developed in Chapter 9.

(1.1) Volitional acts (or responses)

Volitional responses are psychic acts of the will. They are not (affectively) "felt," but are fully within the power of the conscious subject to bring them into existence or not. These responses can either be completely inner, such as when I inwardly say a "yes" or "no" to some state of affairs,[68] but without any further bodily expression or action. An action occurs when someone interiorly decides and then wills to change a fact about the state of the world. While a volitional response can remain completely inner, not leading to action, it can also be an action. Although the interior dimension of willing is always within my conscious power, insofar as I can always inwardly say this "yes" or "no" to any state of affairs, the actual success of being able to change some fact within the world by my action is determined by my actual power, as I might not have the strength, say, to successfully save a person from drowning. And while volitional powers are not "felt," they can be applied against certain feelings or instincts going in the opposite direction that are felt, such as when a person overcomes his fear with his "cold will" to actually attempt a dangerous rescue in turbulent waters.

(1.2) Affective acts (or responses)

Affective responses concern those psychic acts which are essentially "felt," such as with responses of joy, love,* sadness, depression, and so forth.[69] While inner volitional responses are always within our power, affective responses arise spontaneously within the soul (outside our will). And—if these feelings are adequate to their (intentional) object—they also come as gifts. For example, it is one thing to *know* something as good and true, it is another to *will* its existence and flourishing, and it is quite another to then love it from one's *heart*.[70] A heartfelt value response that is adequate to the beloved is a great gift to a lover, which does not necessarily follow from knowing and willing the good and the true.

*IS LOVE REALLY A FEELING?

St. Thomas Aquinas famously asserts that love refers to *willing* the good of another as other. Thus, love for him concerns the will and not a mere feeling of the heart. There is obviously much to be said in support of this characterization. Everyone knows how famously fickle feelings are, while the love that persons have for their beloved has to be far more constant, living through the ups and downs of mere feelings.

However, there is a real affective dimension to love as well, especially with the link between love and happiness, which is the fruit of love. To test this idea, imagine a guy coldly coming up to a girl and saying (through tight lips): *will you marry me? You know my binding myself like this to you is a real sacrifice. But no worries! I have a monster will, and I swear I will be faithful to you!*

Let us further suppose that he is completely steadfast and serious about his will to be faithful; it still remains from another direction manifestly deficient. Here one could ask: what does a woman want? Assuming, of course, good sense, she certainly wants the will of the man to be serious about his promises. But there is something more: she wants the man's heart (the center of our affective life) as well. She wants him to say *I give you not only my will but also my heart! You are the one who makes me happy! Let us rush together to the altar!*

Certainly, persons can be fully married without this further dimension of the heart being involved, such as is typically found with state-sponsored marriages. But even with politically motivated marriages, not only will the couple start their married life from a deep hole; they will also have to try to love in such a way as to eventually secure each other's heart. A marriage without the heart involved is dreadful.

Marriages certainly can be fully enacted without the heart. But the fruit of married love is happiness, and happiness is essentially felt.

All three dimensions—of knowing (via the power of intellect), willing (via the will) and feeling (via the heart)—can to some extent be separated, as a person can know what is good and right without willing it. Someone else can know and will something coldly, but not love it. Then, finally, someone else can know and will and love something because it is beautiful and precious. In this last case—to know, will and love what *is* and what *ought* to be—there is an instance of personal integration,* of wholeness, whereby a person is not at war with one's self, not suppressing or repressing one dimension for the sake of another, but is instead unified and at peace with one's self and with all that is genuinely good and true.

*CAN PERSONAL INTEGRATION BE ACHIEVED BY GLORYING IN EVIL?

At first glance, it would seem so. Someone could say *I hate him. I know what I want, and I wish him dead. Then I will rejoice and dance over his grave!*

Is this an instance of "personal integration"?

I think not. While this evil joy does not go against that person's intellect, will and heart, it does go contrary to his nature. He is built for what is authentically good—for the world of value—and this evil joy contradicts that world and thereby contradicts his nature. Thus, there is not a full and complete integration, as there remains a conflict between person and nature.

Remember again the Beast from the fairytale *Beauty and the Beast*. The Beast, before meeting Belle, had a certain kind of integration of intellect, will and heart. But this integration had a kind of ontological inauthenticity[71] as he was at war with his nature. His nature was really that of a prince, which symbolizes the kind of person he ought to be, the fulfillment of his nature. It was only by his falling in love with Belle that he could identify and then actualize this deeper center of his being. Thus, there is a dovetailing of his true being with his vocation to live up to it.

Affective psychic responses can also go in conflicting directions. Instead of leading to personal integration, they can become divorced from the intellect and will, even from any discernable rational relation to reality and then take on a kind of life of their own. This kind of affective life can then become tyrannical. Instead of right reason and the person's own will being the master of the soul, instinctual urges, addictions and passions take over, dominating the person. This lower nature tyranny can lead to a person's self-destruction, such as when a person knows perfectly well that some dangerous drug can lead to misery and death, and yet yields to the demands of the urge for the drug anyway. Psychologists study people desiring things in a disordered way: of loving the objects of their addictions and vices, putting this "love" even ahead of their own best interests.

2. Products of psychic acts

There is a real distinction between the psychic act of judging and its product, the judgment, as well as between the psychic act of promising and what it produces, the promise. Psychology especially investigates the psychic acts of judging and promising, while the discipline of logic studies the judgment (or propositions) and the discipline of ethics investigates the promise. Both judgments and promises are examples of products of psychic acts. What will be unfolded below are some of the many different kinds of products of psychic acts, some of which are thematic to psychology, especially if they are crucial for our happiness or misery. Now I want to evaluate psychic acts by distinguishing five categories.

(2.1) Intellectual and volitional products of psychic acts[72]

Propositions, convictions, beliefs, and opinions are all examples of products of intellectual psychic acts (or psychic responses). For instance, a proposition is brought into being by an act of judging, while a belief is the product of a psychic act of believing. Both the psychic acts and their products are immaterial in nature, insofar as material predicates—such as being colored, gaseous, circular, or having weight—are inapplicable to both. However, their respective kind of immateriality differs. The first—psychic acts—is a psychological reality in the sphere of real, concrete existence, while the second—their products—refers to sheer abstractions. Thus, propositions and beliefs, as products of psychic acts, are *psychological* only in a derivative way.

Similarly, promises and vows are products of volitional acts. While volitional acts are of primary interest to psychology—insofar as they are essentially conscious—the products of these acts are secondary. This secondary interest may partially explain why some psychologists tend to underestimate them. For example, Carl Rogers prizes becoming over being, especially when that being is merely in the past, such as when someone made a promise or vow in the past. For Rogers, what is important is the present moment in a continual process of volitionally affirming that (past) promise. When the volitional affirmation in the present is missing, the promise made in the past loses its significance.

Naturally, there is a sense in which everything in our experience exists only in the present moment. The past is over, the future is not yet; neither exist in the now. But someone like Rogers seems to imagine the self as existing in the present only in the sense of a continual "new becoming" at each moment, as he emphasizes "becoming" over "being," again discounting all "fixed states." He states, "It seems to me that the good life is not any fixed state. It is not, in my estimation, a state of virtue, or contentment, or nirvana, or happiness."[73] But, what if the person possesses the kind of metaphysical being that exists not only in the present moment, but whose life is also spread out in time (moment-by-moment through time)? Then there would exist two dimensions of a person's being: the first referring to that continual state of "becoming" in each new present moment, and the second to that which "exists" through time.[74] For example, a child—as well as everything else in this world—only exists in the present (first dimension), even though she is substantially the same child at five years as she is at ten years of age (second dimension). One, of course, needs to do justice not just to one or the other, but to both dimensions of time. And both dimensions are verified by our own experience. We are all in the present, and we all remember when we were 5 or 10 years younger.

The earlier topic of the substantial reality of the conscious self can help here, insofar as one further characteristic mark of a substance is that it is the central metaphysical dimension of the being that explains the enduring of that being through time. Most properties (size, shape, weight, etc.) of really existing beings come and go, while the substantial core of that being remains throughout its life.

Consider one psychological consequence that follows: that the person who, for instance, made a serious promise ten years ago is the very same person now. But things like keeping one's promises seem to Rogers to be rigid, "...living in the moment means an absence of rigidity, of tight organization, of the imposition of structure on experience."[75] However, if the substantial reality of the person lives through time, perhaps the obligation to keep one's promises makes more sense. Then things like responsibility and accountability through time will become more real. What if the person has the kind of being that is not exhausted by the present moment?

If a person lives through time, then being true to yourself also includes being true to your promises and vows even though they were made in the past, precisely because—as a simple fact—the embodied self substantially lives through time. Then it is not enough for our beliefs and feelings simply to be our own. Being true to yourself also implies being true to one's own word, even if that word was given in the past.

This analysis is especially relevant with respect to marriage. Given what Rogers has already said above, it is not surprising that he tends to discount marriage vows as well, as he states, "a relationship between a man and a woman is significant, and worth trying to preserve, *only when it is an enhancing, growing experience for each person*" (emphasis added).[76]

Considering the state of marriage and family life in our culture, perhaps the psychological impact of vows could be an area of investigation for psychologists, especially for its power to help overcome loneliness and alienation.

(2.2) Sensible appearances

Psychology is obviously interested in perception, concerning those psychic acts that are oriented towards perceiving material objects: whether as parts or as perceptual wholes (Gestalt psychology), as well as subliminal perception, the limits of perception, and so forth.

An appearance refers to the subjective aspect of the being-that-appears. This aspect, however, is partially constituted by both objective and subjective factors. The objective dimension refers to the thing-in-itself—which is not an appearance—that is grasped through the appearance, such as with our perception of the mountain. The mountain itself is not an appearance; it is rather the thing that appears. The subjective dimension of the appearance is explained by the objective reality of the mountain, of course, but also by the kind of structure of our eyes and our distance from the mountain. Both the objective and subjective dimensions of appearances factor into our experience of the being-that-appears. Thus, in other words, while the appearance of the mountain depends on various objective and subjective factors, the real substantial existence of the mountain is completely independent of any subjective dimension, as the mountain obviously exists in itself whether I perceive it or not.

Thus, to treat the mountain as if it were nothing but an appearance violates our common sense concerning the substantial reality of things. Even thinkers who maintain theoretically (like the philosopher George Berkeley [1685-1753]) that *being is perceiving*[77] must share this common sense on some level, such as when they assume the substantial reality of the trash they take out of their house. That trash is assumed to be something more than a mere appearance.

(2.3) Non-sensible appearances

Besides sensible appearances, there are other kinds of appearances. For example, both foreignness and ancientness are appearances, but they go back to our intellectual understanding of what we experience, as opposed to there being some sensible aspect of the perception itself (as with colors or sounds). Similar to the dimension of substance, these non-sensible appearances intellectually modify our conceptions, such as when we say that the Cambodian culture really is foreign to us. And like sensible appearances, these non-sensible appearances are not completely subjective, insofar as the actual Cambodian culture helps constitute its appearance. While the Cambodian culture really, objectively exists, its cultural quality appears (to most people) as foreign. This foreignness is not completely objective, as nobody would say that the foreignness of the Cambodian culture is intrinsically foreign. It is obviously not foreign to the people of Cambodia. All appearances are like foreignness hybrids—partially objective and partially subjective—and it is this subjective dimension which makes it of interest to psychology, insofar as it is (partially) a product of and dependent upon psychic acts of people from other cultures encountering the Cambodian culture.

(2.4) Pleasure (as an especially important kind of appearance)

Certain sensible things like a Pepsi strike some people as pleasurable. There are also non-sensible realities that are also pleasurable, such as when a person takes pride in his own intellectual abilities. Pleasure possesses a *relational* (as opposed to *intrinsic* importance, characterizing value) importance having the kind of being of an appearance, insofar as things appear differently when they offer the promise of giving pleasure. Using an earlier example, walking into a gym to play basketball, I hardly notice the Pepsi machine. It does not stand out in my perception. But after playing some games, I now see the Pepsi machine in a different way. It is *as if* an inner light emanates from the soda machine beckoning me to buy a drink. And yet, this "inner light" is not experienced as referring to an importance intrinsic to the Pepsi, as if its attractiveness is a fully objective property of its being. It makes no "claim" to objectivity like the value of, say, a person's life and being, which really does make such a claim. Thus, real values are not only *intrinsic* in their nature; they are also experienced as making a "claim" to being fully objective. And, if that value really is what it claims to be, then it possesses a fully objective reality, as opposed to any kind of appearance. Values are not experienced as appearances because appearances do not make any "claim" to objectivity,[78] and so there is nothing to debunk. Values, in contrast, can be debunked, such as when I think some heroic action was performed out of love when it was actually motivated merely to impress someone.

Thus, there are two radically different kinds of importance and motivation. One kind, value importance, is fully objective and thus part of the objective furniture, so to speak, of the world. The second—what was called in Chapter 2 the importance of the subjectively satisfying—is not fully objective, but has a kind of being of an appearance, related specifically to a person's pleasure* (or displeasure concerning the subjectively *dis*satisfying). Because value is a fully objective property of real beings and psychic acts, such phenomena can possess this kind of importance. Beings possessing value not only "exist" but are "worthy to exist." As a result, a person ought to give not just any response but a right, due, adequate response to those beings who possess intrinsic value. Thus, with values we have an intelligible ground or basis for an *ought*.

*A SECOND SENSE OF PLEASURE: AS ACTUAL ENJOYMENT

Up to this point, I have been considering pleasure from the point of view of a kind of (psychic) appearance that can motivate us. The object appears as pleasurable.

There is an obvious second sense of pleasure. This sense does not refer to motivating and anticipating some pleasure that appears, but to the actual enjoyment of the pleasure itself.

In contrast, while nobody says that we "ought" to like Pepsi, everyone ought to respect the intrinsic value of persons. There is no violation of the Pepsi by not liking it in the way that there really is a violation of persons by not respecting them. One could put it this way: in itself, a Pepsi is more or less[79] neutral in importance and only becomes important in relation to persons who like it. But hating blacks and Jews for racist reasons is reprehensible, as they deserve—being human persons—our respect. If possible, we should try to talk people out of their prejudice and racism against any ethnic group, whereas we do not bother trying to get people to like Pepsi.

And, finally, one hardly needs to mention how important pleasure (as well as displeasure) is for a psychology of motivation. This importance can be recognized without maintaining that pleasure or pain is the only source for *all* motivation. This goes too far, as persons can also be motivated by that which is important-in-itself, that is, by intrinsic value.

(2.5) Meaningful "fruits" of psychic acts: depression, hope, despair

If a person gives himself over to superficialities, such as continuous enjoyment and comfort, it would not be surprising to discover this person developing a growing sense of boredom and ennui, a gnawing, growing sense of the meaninglessness of life and existence. Or take another example of a person who has been disappointed in love, and then from that experience has adopted the attitude of being soured about the future possibilities of love, the fruit of which is the further experience of sadness, anger and even despair. Of course, such people do not will these fruits that follow from their freely willed responses and attitudes. They are just the meaningful consequences stemming from certain psychological attitudes that have been adopted.

This fruit is clearly different from a purely causal or "brute" connection—where there is no meaningful relation—say, between some drug and consequent feeling state (whether euphoric or depressive; see below, point 7). Here, in contrast, there is a meaningful, rational connection between triviality and consequent ennui, or between being soured and consequent depression. That triviality leads to boredom "makes sense."

(2.6) Further "fruit" of psychic acts leading to happiness and self-fulfillment

This particular fruit is so foundational that it deserves separate analysis, especially for psychology, which has always been interested in self-actualization and self-fulfillment. What is it that actually fulfills a person?

Aristotle famously answers that it is happiness. But he does not mean by happiness something reducible to a mere feeling. Persons can certainly "feel good"—on some level—from habitually getting drunk or doing serious drugs, but they are hardly fulfilling themselves in any serious sense. Such people are, in fact, actually going in an opposite direction toward eventual ruination and misery. For instead of coming to a right relation to reality—to what is and to what ought to be—which is a condition for the possibility of genuine happiness, they are fleeing from it. In contrast, Aristotle speaks of that happiness which comes from the fulfillment and fruit of our rational nature, that is, of being in a right relation to reality.

It is worthwhile noting the paradoxical character of self-fulfillment. This state is, oddly enough, not achieved by making it the end of a person's motivation, with everything else serving merely as means. That approach involves putting one's self at the center and theme of all activities and motivation, which seems close to the topic discussed earlier (Chapter 4) of an immature self-absorption. This implies being disrespectful towards other persons who should never be used merely as means for our own ends, including the end of our own self-fulfillment. Rather, one needs to find out what is genuinely true and good*— such as the intrinsic value of other persons—and then respond adequately to them for their sake. This obviously involves not only a self-gift, but also a certain self-forgetfulness, where the focus is on others and not one's self. The result of this outward (transcendent) direction of the self towards truth and goodness leads to a deepening of the self, leading (again paradoxically) to self-discovery and even to self-fulfillment. Self-fulfillment does not lie exclusively within the orbit of the self—as if the secret to life is somehow being "true" to your own ever-changing feelings—but rather in responding adequately to reality, especially to what is most important.

*ANOTHER POSSIBLE "FRUIT" OF PSYCHIC ACTS: MISERY

What happens if a person turns away from *what is genuinely true and good*?

Take, for example, a case of those people who live for themselves. Such persons are obviously selfish, looking at the world through the prism of their own self-centeredness. Naturally, they can also be congenial and friendly, but only in circumstances that align with their own narrow self-interest. Instead of interpreting some situation according simply to the facts—including value facts—such people will inevitably interpret them only according to their pleasures. This approach can characterize individual actions, as well as whole personalities.

What is the "fruit" of this kind of approach? I suggest it is one of frustration and eventual misery. Animals are not built for truth and goodness, but persons are. People who are self-enclosed are frustrating their own self-fulfillment, independent of whether they recognize this fact or not.

(2.7) Imaginative objects and illusions

Both imaginative objects and illusions are intentional—in the sense of being objects of consciousness, insofar as they are "about something" (Chapter 4)—even though they are not themselves "real" in the sense of having an independent, transcendent reality (in the sense of having an objective existence "in themselves") going beyond the conscious subject. Their unreality might make one hesitate to see them as any kind of suitable object of scientific inquiry. And yet, Freud might very well be right in thinking that they can provide a kind of window into a person's unconscious life, as he makes a surprisingly strong argument for this position in his book, *The Interpretation of Dreams.*

It is worth distinguishing between the psychic reality of imaginative objects (such as the magical creatures from the Harry Potter novels), illusions, and appearances (2.2, 2.3 and 2.4 above). Imaginative objects and illusions are not partially produced by and relative to both the experiencing subject and some object, like appearances. They are rather completely produced by the subject—existing only at the mercy of the subject—without any objective dimension whatsoever. While imaginative objects are the products of volitional acts producing them, illusions simply come spontaneously, such as when dreaming. We do not *will to dream;* we simply dream. Dreams and illusions come from outside of one's will, as are sometimes an effect of some bio-chemical cause, as for instance from hallucinogenic drugs.

Furthermore, imaginative objects are similar to appearances insofar as they do not make any "claim" to objectivity, while illusory objects do make such a claim, which is why we wake up in a cold sweat from a nightmare of monsters chasing us. Thus, for instance, the appearance of the "goodness" of the Pepsi merely goes back to the way it is experienced by those who take pleasure in it. Nobody thinks this "goodness" has the importance of intrinsic value (that is, as being fully objective). Nor does the pleasure of the Pepsi have the kind of being of a mere illusion (being fully subjective) either. It rather has the being of an appearance (being partially subjective and partially objective).

After discussing psychic acts and seven different kinds of products of psychic acts, I want to turn to other basic kinds of objects that psychology investigates.

3. Patterns of thinking and feeling

Psychic acts—especially those acts that are essentially felt (such as joy, delight, sadness, depression, etc.), together with the various products of all psychic acts (such as conviction, doubt, belief, etc.)—can not only be investigated singly, they also reveal patterns. Some patterns of thinking/willing/feeling are adaptive, open and adequate to reality, both to what is and to what ought to be, that is, to what is true and genuinely good. Others are maladaptive, enclosed within themselves, inadequate to what is true and good and, ultimately, self-destructive.

Here I am obviously not thinking of innocent theoretical errors about reality, like when someone occasionally gets their sums wrong, but rather to those patterns of thinking and willing that especially reveal ongoing misinterpretations of reality. But instead of learning from mistakes, those suffering from them will sometimes distressingly "double down," repeating over and over again the same mistake. One wonders, why is that? What is the psychological benefit that accrues from repeating these kinds of mistakes? The person suffering from them will blame everything and everyone else—except the actual maladaptive pattern itself—which is not only given a free pass but also is often hardly noticed. If it is noticed, it is typically explained away. Even if a proper understanding of the true nature of the misery of these patterns is grasped, escaping them remains difficult.

Within this broad, general category of maladaptive patterns of thinking and willing, there are more specific sub-patterns that coalesce, such as obsessive-compulsive disorders, anxiety, depression, schizophrenia, and many others, which the science of personality disorders can identify and unfold. These more specific kinds of disorders need to be empirically observed and classified. One common denominator for all of them concerns the degree of the rationality (or irrationality) of the person. If a person's "hold" on reality is weak, think of neurosis; if severe, psychosis.

Psychologists have also tried to identify those patterns of thinking and feeling that are rational, healthy, and adequate to reality. Humanistic psychologists, such as Carl Rogers, Abraham Maslow, and more recently Martin Seligman, have tried to identify those patterns that are self-actualizing and self-fulfilling. In the next section, I also want to contribute to this "positive psychology" of fulfillment by discussing morally good habits.

4. Character formation: including moral habits

Some patterns of acting have an impact upon our character. It is not just substantial realities—like persons and mountains—that can live through time, but also certain psychic attitudes can also live consciously, albeit implicitly, through time. For example, if a person is in love with his wife, one could rightly say that he loves her even when he is not explicitly thinking of her. Let us say, for example, that he at one particular time during the day is consumed by the work of his job. Even during those times, one might notice a certain happy quality about him. There is a bounce in his step. He is in love, and he knows that he in turn is loved. This love implicitly "colors" and "tones" his whole conscious life. One could say that his love for his spouse is like a prism through which he then sees reality. This prism need not itself be directly reflected upon or even at times noticed by him. Of course, he could go on to actualize his love explicitly by thinking about her, so there is nothing repressive (as if by continually forcing some content out of his conscious life) during those intervals when this awareness of his love is merely implicit. Although, if he does not periodically actualize his love for her explicitly and thematically, this love will eventually fade. Furthermore, the reality of this love could easily have a certain moral quality to it, helping to form this person's character towards moral soundness.

Something similar, unfortunately, works in reverse with depression and despair.[80] Although these states need not have a moral quality, someone in despair will be "under a cloud." This state—similar to the above example of love—will also live *through* time, even during those times in which someone is thinking about something else. It is not merely localized in consciousness, as if it only exists when thinking explicitly about one's own depression and despair. Other people will often notice this despair as it can be unconsciously expressed (whether repressed or not) through one's body—by his or her slouching, drooping demeanor—even when one is preoccupied with other activities.

Anger can also be formative of character. But in contrast to despair,* anger can at times be localized only to particular situations, such as when I overhear a friend making a slighting comment about me. At the moment of hearing it, I am upset. But that anger can pass, if for example the person making such comments apologizes, or I recognize the truth of the criticism. Of course, my anger can be justifiable—such as when the slighting comment was unfair to me—and at other times not. Either way, there is a temptation to come to enjoy this experience of anger—of the feeling of righteous indignation—and even come to encourage that feeling in other situations. If this is done too much, a person could develop a habit of anger, taking on a psychological life of its own. That is, the initial intentional character of the particular feeling to its respective object (motivating the anger) will tend to weaken over time, as the inward psychic poison of the anger will start spreading out into the whole *psyche,* eventually poisoning its host. Then instead of being temporarily *angry over something,* a person can become—as a character trait, in general and over time—just *angry,* even though that anger will typically be implicit, just beneath the surface, waiting for an opportunity or excuse to become explicit and then explode. In fact, this kind of person will often look for an object which then functions as a scapegoat for that generalized anger. The scapegoat functions to "justify and explain" the anger, even though the true source of the anger lies elsewhere. Anger, after all, can be enjoyed as well as pleasure. So, just as love can become a prism through which one can see the world, so can anger.

*DESPAIR—AS OPPOSED TO ANGER— CANNOT BE LOCALIZED IN TIME

While anger can be localized to particular situations—such as when my anger is strictly tied to some object motivating that anger—despair is not. It is rather essentially "spread out," so to speak, through time.

Someone could object and say, *No! the reason for my despair is completely explained by the fact* (localized to a set time) *that my girlfriend left me.* Soren Kierkegaard (1813-1855), the father of modern existentialism, responds, "With despair it is different. As soon as despair manifests itself in a person, it is manifest that the person **was** in despair. … For in case the condition comes about which brings him to despair, it is at that same moment manifest that he has been in despair throughout the whole of his previous life" [emphasis added].[81]

The stronger the habit—for example, anger—the less provocation it takes to elicit it. As just noted, such people will often (sub-consciously) look for excuses to be provoked, not only from minor provocations but also from no real provocation at all. It is as if this (implicit) habit of anger has developed a kind of psychological dynamism that is looking to be explicitly expressed. This habit of the poison of anger could become so strong as to become the dominant note of a personality.

There exists a real dynamism within psychological character habits, whether for good or for ill, to "break out" and be expressed. For example, another person could develop a habit of generosity towards others. This person, similar in one sense to the angry guy looking to express his anger, will also look for ways to actualize his generosity. All these kinds of habits (such as of anger, generosity, and love), even when implicit, will still have a dynamic quality about them, insofar as they will be looking for outward and explicit expression. During those times when not outwardly expressed, a person's ingrained habit of anger, love or despair will never quite leave them, hanging on implicitly to "tone" or "color" a person's whole conscious life.

One might contrast these character traits (including moral character traits) that can implicitly live through time with other conscious acts that cannot do this. For example, I can be explicitly and consciously aware of the simple equation that *2+2=4*. It can also exist passively in memory, as this simple fact is constantly available to us in memory. But, when passive in memory, notice how it does not "color" our conscious experience. It is simply absent. It is not like anger or generosity, which, even when not explicitly experienced, can still implicitly influence a person's conscious life. Why is that? One central reason lies in the fact that *2+2=4* lacks the significance to influence a person's life through time. In contrast, with the loving husband, his awareness that he is loved really is significant. This awareness can not only be explicitly consciously experienced and not only exist in memory; it can also live implicitly "coloring" our conscious life through time.

The strength of these habits enduring through time increases, whether for good or for ill,* every time they are actualized by being expressed. Thus, the angry guy will be more and more unable to deal with and overcome this vice, especially since by feeding his anger, he makes it stronger. A proper psychological strategy for extinction within the soul is not any kind of actualization, including even "righteous indignation," but rather starvation. This person needs to stop getting angry or at least to will to stop being angry, even when he wants to and even if his anger in some particular situation is actually justified.

*BAD HABITS COME EASY; GOOD HABITS COME HARD

Ever notice how building a house is hard and expensive, while burning one down is quick and easy, taking hardly more than a match? This is similar to moral habit formation. Bad habits come quickly. Good habits are hard to develop.

Habit starvation, unfortunately, also works for one's virtues as well. One way of falling out of love or losing the virtue of generosity is not by actualizing it explicitly in consciousness, and by not putting that love or generosity into action. To maintain and to grow in these virtues, one needs to practice them.

The effect of such practices is the formation of what can be called a moral character. Although we are not free to directly will a good character—as I can no more directly will a good moral character, say, of a great saint than I can "jump to the moon"—we are free to directly will individual good actions and appropriate inner responses, which in turn organically develop good character. Thus, the kind of freedom at stake with moral habits is indirect. It is this indirect link to freedom that makes us responsible for the kind of character we develop, even though we cannot directly will it. And just as there is a connection between freedom and character, so is there one between character and a person's affective response. Granted that both character and affective responses are outside our direct freedom. We can, however, indirectly will them by directly willing those individual acts and responses that in turn build them up. Then notice what happens: when a morally good character develops, the proper affective response associated with that virtue will also organically develop. In fact, one sign of an ordered moral character is the presence of appropriate affective responses.

Persons make decisions and choices through their own free action; as a result of their actions, their own character is wrought. This character is explained in and through freedom, both directly and indirectly.

5. Social relations and behavior

Social psychology attempts to discern and understand patterns of social interactions between persons. How is it that persons can influence each other? Earlier in this chapter, I mentioned how persons ought to treat each other: as ends in themselves and never merely as means.

There are two basic ways in which persons can influence each other. First, there is what can be called the "Madison Avenue" approach, that is, through the world of advertising, ideology* and behavioristic manipulation of others. Secondly, one can influence others by what we can term the "Socratic approach," that is, by trying to help people see the truth of some intellectual position for themselves and then invite them to respond adequately to it. For, after all, Socrates was not merely interested in "The Truth," he was interested in people seeing what is true for themselves, that is, *with their own eyes*. It is not enough for persons to merely give *The Right Answer*. Even if this answer is true, they also need to see the truth for themselves.

*IDEOLOGY

Occasionally some university professor is in the news for trying to manipulate students into agreement with his or her social, metaphysical or political agenda. This manipulation could be carried out via ridicule, threats, name-calling or shame. Naturally, professors have a right to give examinations on material appropriate to the theme of the class. Still, it is one thing to require students to learn the arguments; it is quite another to insist that students accept them as true. For a professor to insist upon agreement from students is illegitimate. Of course, a teacher can and should give arguments and evidence for the truth of his or her position. But a real teacher needs to appeal to students through their freedom, and students have to be free to evaluate the truth of an argument via insight and proof. There needs to be, in other words, evidence as opposed to any manipulation or force. To approach some academic subject matter—either from professors or students—from any other point of view besides truth and evidence is disastrous for the liberal arts, leading to substitution of mere ideology and mere indoctrination for a true philosophical spirit. A true philosophical spirit requires freedom.

Notice how in helping one see something true, there has to be a complete absence of manipulation—typifying the first approach—and the corresponding respect for both the independent minds of others as well as for truth. Furthermore, while a manipulative approach leads to subservience, the Socratic approach leads to independence. As C. S. Lewis puts it,

> Where the old initiated, the new merely 'conditions.' The old dealt with its pupils as grown birds deal with young birds when they teach them to fly: the new deals with them more as the poultry-keeper deals with young birds—making them thus or thus for purposes of which the birds know nothing. In a word, the old was a kind of propagation—men transmitting manhood to men: the new is merely propaganda.[82]

A real teacher then is like an old bird teaching a young bird how to fly. When they learn to think for themselves, they become independent of the teacher. That is exactly what real teachers want, and what propagandists and manipulators fear.

Furthermore, the Socratic approach also dovetails with the value responding attitude (from point 4 above). Treating people as ends and not merely as means has a rebound effect on those acting in that way, insofar as they not only become more receptive towards others, but also become better persons as well.

6. Bodily behavioral patterns

As already noted, the term *behavior* has both a meaning specific to psychology as well as a very broad, general meaning, referring to how any being acts in the world, given its particular nature. What makes behavior in this general sense specifically psychological is its relation to conscious life. Even if one assumes that the soul is substantially distinct from the body—as opposed to being a mere property of it (Chapter 4)—the soul is also immersed in the body in such a way that a new substantial being is constituted: a human being, body and soul.[83] This mutual immersion of body and soul allows for their intimate union, insofar as the soul remains a relatively distinct phenomenon even while it forms the body into the unity of the human person. It is this unity that makes for the possibility of the body being expressive of inner psychic acts.

Furthermore, psychic states—this time expressed through a person's body and behavior—can be understood because they follow patterns (similar to point 3 above, concerning *patterns of thinking and feeling*), and these expressive patterns can be understood.* Everyone knows how a person's actual behavior can sometimes be a better guide to his or her inner life than what they actually say. Although there are also obvious limitations here, as we can often successfully hide what we are inwardly thinking and feeling from being expressed outwardly. We all can be good actors, even performing actions that go in a very different direction than what we are actually feeling or experiencing.

*THE INTELLIGIBILITY OF BODILY EXPRESSION IS NOT REDUCIBLE TO MERE BEHAVIORAL CONDITIONING

Sometimes behaviorists will theorize that *all* bodily expression is exclusively learned via conditioning principles. With this idea, the baby is a kind of "blank slate," and socialization is completely explained in terms of the principle of association, with differing kinds of behavior becoming over time associated with differing inner psychic meanings.

This view goes against the notion that we can directly intuit certain psychic states and that there is an intelligible connection between certain bodily expressions and inner psychic states. It also follows from this behavioristic interpretation that certain bodily expressions would then not be cross-cultural. All bodily expression would go back to cultural conditioning, which is culture-specific.

It is quite possible to accept the reality of a limited cultural conditioning without asserting that all human expression is reducible to mere conditioning.

One evidence for the position that we can directly intuit certain inner psychic states via bodily expression is to consider an example of a place seen by many millions of people from practically every culture across the span of centuries. Think, for example, of the Sistine Chapel in Vatican City. Specifically, consider the back wall of that Chapel, the location of Michelangelo's famous *Last Judgement.* If you know the painting, you know there are people depicted going up to heaven as well as others going to hell. All these people will have correspondingly different expressions, some with hope and happiness, others with misery and despair.

Now imagine this experiment: of showing a small child, just old enough to be able to focus sufficient to see those faces in the painting but before much enculturation, of those in despair. That despair is clearly "written on their face," and a child seeing it would not like it. The reverse is true for those being saved.

And it is not just babies. Dogs do not seem to be able to grasp the intelligible meaning found in paintings, but they are capable of intuiting the emotional state of their master, as a dog will at times try to comfort a depressed and miserable master.

Bodily behavior is clearly important for psychology because of its link to a person's inner conscious life. However, if the center of psychology lies with conscious life, then bodily behavior is a step removed from that center. This may be surprising, given the fact that behavior is so emphasized in modern psychology. Why does contemporary psychology sometimes confuse what is central to psychology, conscious life, with what is theoretically more secondary, behavior?

Influencing the behavior of others can obviously have tremendous benefits for those interested in power and control. There is nothing necessarily illegitimate about that interest, especially if it serves the common good. One theoretical difficulty, however, is with confusing what is central to psychology, elucidating conscious life, while overemphasizing what is theoretically important but of secondary interest, such as behavior.*

*HOW THE THEORETICAL AND THE PRACTICAL CAN WORK TOGETHER

An orientation toward the practical is obviously found in contemporary psychology. This is clearly a cultural trend and not localized to psychology. While the ancients especially emphasized the theoretical over the practical, or truth over usefulness, this emphasis is typically reversed today (try applying for a grant that has no practical usefulness).

It is, however, not necessary to choose one over the other as we can have both. In fact, one excellent thing to do for the sake of innovation and technology is to emphasize pure science, which is only interested in the truth about physical or psychological reality. Notice that the moment pure science atrophies, innovation similarly decreases because so many practical applications come from people doing pure science, without necessarily recognizing or predicting the practical significance of their work.[84] Since it is not always possible to see where innovation is to be found, let us do pure science whose object simply is truth, and then innovations will come.

Sometimes understanding and charting bodily behavior can become the central or even exclusive theme of psychological investigation, which is the focus of the psychological school of behaviorism.*

*ONE VARIANT OF BEHAVIORISM THAT EXPLICITLY DENIES CONSCIOUS EXPERIENCE

Consider someone like the behaviorist John Watson (1878–1958), who denied the real existence of inner conscious states. He states,

> From the time of Wundt on, consciousness became the keynote of psychology. It is the keynote of all psychologies today except behaviorism. It [consciousness] is a plain assumption just as improvable, just as unapproachable as the old concept of soul. And to the behaviorist, the two terms are essentially identical, so far as concerns their metaphysical implications.[85]

If consciousness is identical to soul, then a denial of soul is obviously a denial of consciousness. He continues by noting that no one has "touched a soul, or has seen one in a test tube, or has in any way come into relationship with it as he has with the other objects of his daily experience. With the development of the physical sciences which came with the Renaissance, a certain release from the stifling soul cloud was obtained."[86] Certainly, Watson's solution in one sense solves the problem of the empirical method needing to be ordered to immaterial, private conscious acts: he just denies their existence. But the problem with this "solution" is that it contradicts obvious experiential (even if non-empirical) facts, which he himself oddly presupposes...even in the above quotes. For his own act of denying conscious acts itself presupposes an inner conscious act of denying. This is similar to his conscious act of making an assumption (as he plainly asserts in the block quote just above), making Watson's assertion incoherent.

What especially interests me about this passage is Watson's motivation for this rather surprising move. Why does he feel the necessity to deny conscious life, which is so obvious and self-evident? Perhaps it is because he senses its incompatibility with the idea of his radical behaviorism, which claims to be the exclusive object of all psychological investigation. Since conscious life is not an object of sense perception—

obviously crucial to the behavioristic method—he denies conscious life. Thus, he gives us a kind of negative affirmation of one of the central theses of this book: that psychological empiricism cannot explain all psychological phenomena. If he accepted conscious life, he would then have to admit limitations to his behaviorism.

Just because behavior is not everything in psychology does not mean it is nothing, as it is typically an expression of our inner conscious life. There are, however, instances in which behavior can become relatively unhinged from inner conscious experiences. For example, think of learning how to ride a bicycle. At first, we will concentrate hard on maintaining our balance. But over time, as we acquire that habit, this conscious need to maintain balance will tend to disappear. So now we can focus on other things, such as the joy of riding the bike for fun. And certainly, behavioristic principles concerning habits can be applied to an almost infinite number of other instances, from bike riding to shopping to voting to friends, etc. In all such instances, patterns or habits are developed, which can then be studied by behavioral psychologists, with the corresponding link to conscious activity being correspondingly less thematic.

These behavioral habits are in one respect very different from the moral character habits discussed above (point 4). Acts building moral character lead to an *increase* of consciousness* in ways that correspond to them, such as, for instance, a generous person will be more consciously attentive to the needs of others. Even when these moral habits are not explicitly expressed, they remain implicitly active, "coloring" our conscious experience, not only living through time but also acting as a prism through which we see and then interact with reality. And with moral habits, the stronger the habit, the stronger the consequent conscious coloring. In contrast, with (non-moral) behavior-oriented habits—such as with the above example of riding a bike—the link connecting them to psychic acts is far less apparent and thematic. In fact, the stronger the habit, the more there is a *decrease* in awareness of inner psychic experience.

*ONE PSYCHOLOGY TEXTBOOK WRITER ON CONSCIOUSNESS OF SELF

One well-known introductory psychology textbook writer, David Myers, states, "Tibetan Buddhists deep in meditation and Franciscan nuns deep in centering prayer report a diminished sense of self, space, and time."[87] This seems to contradict my claim that in giving an adequate response to all values, including moral values, there is a greater conscious sense of self.

Perhaps this seeming contradiction with Myers' text can be resolved by going back to an earlier distinction between intentional self-reflection and lateral self-presence (Chapter 4). From the point of view of intentional self-reflection, there is with something like prayer a decrease of self-consciousness. This is obviously true, as the "theme" of prayer is certainly not the self. But with lateral self-presence, there is with "centering prayer" an increase of self-awareness because of this greater self-presence. Persons will naturally come to themselves and become "centered" when in the presence of something great and magnificent. David Myers does not have this theoretical notion of self-presence, so he misses that link to our conscious life.

It is especially with these behaviorally-oriented habits that we can better understand B. F. Skinner's thinking that conscious experience is irrelevant to his radical behaviorism. He wants to predict and structure habit formation, and he is not too picky about whether the person he is trying to behaviorally "shape" is aware of the manipulation involved.[88] In contrast, the situation is reversed when it comes to moral character formation, and actual behavior is the less important factor. For example, imagine the earlier example of playing a game with someone intentionally trying to trip me, but failing in the attempt. That is very different from a second instance of a person not trying to hurt an opponent, even if—inadvertently—he does so. I rightly blame the first person—even though he did not hurt me and not the second, while he is the one who did the damage. In both cases, what really counts is the (inner psychic) intent and not the behavioral effect. But with radical behaviorism, as well as habit formation in general, what counts is not the inner psychological experience, but the presence of the actual habit formed.

Everyone knows how advantageous it is to be able to control behavior, as it leads to the increased power of being able to manipulate others for one's own ends: to sell some product or acquire votes for political power. Cynics think that truth and argumentation are merely reducible to such manipulation. It is crucially important for psychology to distinguish between using psychological techniques for manipulating others—even assuming the best of motivations from the behaviorists—and appealing to others because some position is true and authentically good. Ultimately, it is to everyone's advantage to treat others as persons by making arguments that appeal to their intellects and wills, as opposed to merely treating them as if they were mere pawns on a chessboard to be manipulated. And no one should write off an interest in truth as being hopelessly naïve, as this approach destroys all science, including the science of behaviorism.

It is hardly necessary to point out how often people disrespect truth—either by ignoring it or by hypocritically trying to fool others and even themselves by merely paying lip service to it—especially when the call to respect it goes against their own self-interest. All this is granted. The point here is not whether we in fact live in a right relation to truth, but whether we as human beings possess the basic ontological power—missing in animals—to know it. And if we possess the power to know truth, it is worthwhile reflecting upon its psychological significance (Chapter 8), especially if it is instrumental to the fulfillment of our nature. All this remains true even while granting how relatively seldom a right relation to truth and authentic goodness is actually achieved.

If psychologists exclusively focus on behavioral control, they will inevitably come to a skewed notion of the human person, and therefore of psychology. Psychology will then only focus on our lower nature, oriented exclusively to manipulation and power for the fulfillment of our instincts and needs, and then correspondingly ignore or even deny our higher nature, oriented to what is authentically good and true. This is a fundamental misperception of human nature.

7. Causes and conditions of psychic acts

Psychology is not only interested in the psychic, embodied self, as well as psychic acts and various kinds of products of psychic acts and the body as expressive of them; it is also interested in the causes and conditions for these acts. Interest in these causes and conditions is, of course, also related to biology, specifically to brain physiology and biochemistry. Here one can remember that psychic phenomena, while immaterial, are also embodied by being expressed in and through the body, insofar as the soul is joined to its body, constituting the whole human person. Psychology is obviously interested in the body/soul composite, especially how the body influences the soul, and vice versa.

What is a cause? A cause refers to a power *through which* some change occurs. This differs from a mere condition or enabling factor. A condition is that *without which* something else cannot be or become.* For example, the cause of a snow avalanche could be some loud noise, but the condition for the possibility of that event happening is the recent large amounts of snowfall in some mountainous region.

*CONFUSING CAUSES AND CONDITIONS WITH FREEDOM AND KNOWLEDGE

Not only is there a difference between a cause and a condition, there is also an important difference between two kinds of cause: a caused cause (or secondary cause) and a first cause (personal freedom). There is a temptation within contemporary psychology to confuse both sets of relations. Let us note here one instance of this, going back again to a popular introductory psychology text from David Myers. He states,

> No principle is more central to today's psychology, or to this book, than this: Everything psychological is simultaneously biological. Your every idea, every mood, every urge is a biological happening. You love, laugh, and cry with your body. Without your body—*your genes, your brain, your appearance*—*you are, indeed, nobody.* Although we find it convenient to talk separately of *biological and psychological influences on behavior,* we need to remember: to *think, feel, or act* without a body would be like running without legs [emphasis added].[89]

Notice in this passage there is no reference to freedom. The implication may be that freedom is nothing but a quaint, old-fashioned notion, having no place in a rigorous, scientific setting. A careful scientific explanation will not reference freedom, but rather "biological and psychological influences on behavior."

However, I want to show that once a distinction is made between a condition from a cause—with freedom being one kind of cause, an uncaused cause—there can be room for both science and the possibility of psychic freedom, as well as the personal self who can freely act.

The truth from the above Myers' quote is seen once one identifies "your genes, your brain" as empirically necessary conditions for "think[ing], feel[ing], or act[ing]." For no thinking or willing is possible without the proper operation of your biology and biochemistry. They are obvious necessary conditions without which these activities become impossible. But that does not mean that our biology and biochemistry are the cause of our thinking and acting. In other words, just because something is a condition for something else does not make it a cause for that something else. For example, just because a certain brain temperature range is an empirically necessary condition for thinking clearly does not mean it is the cause of my thinking, much less can it explain the adequacy of the content of my thought. What really explains the adequacy of my thinking, for instance, is that *2+2=4* is the insight into the fact that this sum really does equal *4.* The adequacy of this thought does not go back to biology but to the basic intelligibility of mathematics.

This rather obvious distinction between these two sets of relations—between causes and conditions on the one hand, and the two different kinds of causes (freedom as a first or uncaused cause, versus secondary causation, referring to a caused cause), on the other—is nowhere discussed by Myers. Because he does not distinguish them, he leaves students reading his text to conclude that "your genes, your brain" (for "you are, indeed, nobody") is not only the cause of your thinking, feeling and acting, but also the full explanation for the being of your conscious self. This implication is false.

If Myers is correct and our thinking is merely biologically caused, why does anyone bother with evidence, proof, argument and truth? Then what we think is nothing but an effect of bio-chemical, causal chains. Furthermore, if without these bodily activities "you are, indeed, nobody," how does this not inevitably lead to despair?

One can now apply this distinction between causes and conditions to psychology by comparing something which really is a biological cause or a condition for psychic acts, with other biological events which are not. Recall that a wish or thought may be either conscious or unconscious. But even if unconscious, they still can be oriented towards consciousness and thereby be proper objects of psychological investigation. In contrast, blood circulation and brain synapses are neither conscious, nor are they oriented towards consciousness. They are, therefore, *non*-conscious (as opposed to *un*conscious states,[90] which are still oriented towards consciousness), and in that respect, are not themselves proper or direct objects of psychological investigation.

However, some biological processes might become objects of psychological investigation in a derivative sense if they serve either as conditions or causes of conscious events. Naturally, if biological processes have no relation to psychic phenomena, they are not proper objects of psychology. Thus, psychology is rightly interested in physiology to help explain the conscious processes of perception and biochemistry to explain why certain drugs are consciously experienced as psychedelic or mood-altering. Biological processes must have some link to conscious life to be of interest to psychology; otherwise, there is no distinguishing psychology from biology.

When it comes to understanding biological and biochemical causes and conditions for psychic experiences, the empirical, scientific method is clearly to be preferred. Some objects are suitable to the empirical method, while others are ordered more to a philosophical investigation.

8. Psychology of learning[91]

In this section, I want to distinguish two basic kinds of learning: empirical or intellectual, and then show how they interrelate to each other.

Although processes like blood circulation and heart arrhythmia are not directly and primarily suitable objects of psychological investigation—as they are obviously biological realities only tangentially (at best) related to consciousness—they are also not fully suitable for a philosophical investigation either because they lack the kind of intelligibility* needed for purely intellectual analysis. This is why we need empirical investigation, as I have to empirically observe the various kinds of links between brain functioning and conscious life in order to know them. I cannot just "close my eyes," so to speak, and see with the "eye of my mind" such links (in the way that I really do intellectually intuit—absolutely and in principle—that *responsibility presupposes freedom*). Concerning purely empirical investigations, a method of sense observation (or empirical intuition) and inductive generalization must be used, as otherwise, I cannot get to a general species understanding (such as the general nature of individual zebras [Chapter 6]). But no inductive generalization is needed with respect to the insight that *2+2=4* because the intuition into these numbers extends to their universal essence structure. Thus, we see—absolutely and in principle—that *2+2* must equal *4*.

*INTELLIGIBILITY

So far in this text, only one criterion (or measure) was explicitly mentioned for an object being suitable for philosophical investigation: that it be somehow (directly or indirectly) given in our common, lived experience, as opposed to some specialized intuition or revelation. This, however, is not the only requirement. Some phenomenon must not only be publicly given in principle to our natural reason, it must also possess an especially *high* level of inner meaningfulness and knowability, which is what I mean by intelligibility.

Intelligibility can be of three differing kinds.[92] First, there is the extremely weak inner meaningfulness of a scribble, which is so little understandable because there is little to understand, and this is because of its almost complete arbitrariness of the direction of its lines. Secondly, there is the intelligibility of, say, a watch, where the parts are intelligibly fitted into a whole for a particular end or purpose, such as that of keeping time. A watch can be understood, with respect to how it works, because of this increased inner meaningfulness. Although even here there is some arbitrariness to it, insofar as there are different ways in which it can be constructed to keep time. Then, thirdly, there are beings which are so intelligible that they in principle cannot be otherwise. For example, once we grasp what responsibility is, we can then "see"—in the sense of intellectually understand via intellectual intuition—its inner intelligible structure such that it simply (or necessarily) cannot exist outside of freedom. Thus, it belongs to the (universal) nature or essence of responsibility to necessarily presuppose freedom. It then is not just this instance of responsibility that presupposes freedom, but *all* instances of it, absolutely and in principle.

Philosophy especially deals with this third kind of intelligibility, while the empirical sciences deal only with the second kind. And, of course, there is no science of the scribble because of its arbitrariness and impoverished intelligibility.

It is worthwhile noting that there are also many objects of psychological investigation that are outside of the philosophical method: such as the different kinds of mental illness, learning theory, perception and developmental psychology, and so forth. One gets at these realities empirically—via the second kind of intelligibility utilizing observation and induction—and not from a philosophical approach.

Only personal beings possess the capacity to grasp the intelligible natures of individual things—both empirically (scientifically) and philosophically—in the (intellectual) "light"* of their universal essence. For if you know something about a species—that is, considered as a universal—you can get a pretty good idea of the state and nature of the individual. You can then come to know, for instance, if this particular individual is healthy or sick, young or old, big or small, in relation to its general species. There is a tremendous advantage to being able to grasp an individual thing in light of its respective universal.

*PSYCHOLOGICAL EVIDENCE FOR INTELLECTUAL LIGHT

Is there psychological evidence for the non-reductive character of intellectual "light" going beyond sensory experience and association? One such evidence comes from the experience of Helen Keller, who, as a 19-month-old baby, contracted a high fever, the result of which left her blind, deaf and mute for the rest of her life. For the next five years, before meeting her teacher (Annie Sullivan), Paul Vitz notes that "She had no serious communication with anyone, even her parents. She was essentially an intelligent but wild high-level primate."[93] However, she came to understand—as a sudden insight—the link between "Her sensory experience…of water on the one hand and on the other the tactile code for water. At that moment, she transcended the two separate but associated experiences and knew that w-a-t-e-r was the name of what she was sensing…she spoke of this as "a strange, new light", this was presumably not a visual light but a kind of "intellectual light…[a] sudden irruption of symbolic thought."[94]

Intellectual intuition is the highpoint of this intellectual light, while the naming that Hellen Keller describes above is only at its beginning. Naming, however, leads to the discovery of the transcendence of the world, which in turn leads to the self-discovery of an inner conscious life and to the distinction between inner from outer, or immanent and transcendent (going beyond the inner self). Developmental psychologists have always known that the discovery of one's own self always lags behind the prior discovery of the world. Both discoveries—of the world and of the self—in turn lead to the possibility of the further light of understanding via intellectual intuition.

In contrast, higher-order animals can "figure stuff out" only on a very concrete (that is, strictly individual) level, without the intellectual "light" of any universal understanding.[95] This concrete rationality is useful for ambushing prey or using sticks as tools to get at food, but only persons can understand individual beings in the intellectual light of their respective general essence structures. Thus, only a person can know what an animal, an ambush, or a tool is, that is, from the point of view of their universal essence structure and meaning.* As a result, the world of a pure animal is actually unimaginably dark (from the point of view of intelligibility), even though some animals possess this concrete kind of rationality and can undoubtedly (sensibly) see or hear better than human beings.

*THE SIGNIFICANCE OF UNDERSTANDING INDIVIDUAL THINGS IN THE "LIGHT" OF THEIR UNIVERSAL ESSENCES

Try this thought experiment: imagine for a moment another person you know. With this concrete image of that person in mind, now abstract (or separate out) from any consideration of this person any understanding of him or her *as a person…as a male (or female)…as a human being…as a college student…as an American…as a being,* including all other considerations that refer to universals. No doubt—if you seriously and consistently get rid of all such universal understandings—your reaction will be this: *without this intellectual "light" of universal understanding, I cannot really even know this individual person at all. In fact, I cannot know anything at all!* Yes, exactly. And yet, this is precisely the situation of any pure animal. They, of course, possess the sense perception of really existing, individual material beings. And they even possess a limited rationality, as noted above, of being able to use sticks as tools or set up ambushes. But any kind of understanding of some being or situation—in the intellectual light of universal essences—is beyond their power. Thus, the kind of rationality pure animals possess is very concrete, limited only within the sphere of concrete instances.

In fact, pure perception alone—without this intellectual light—is not yet even knowledge. It is the "matter," so to speak, of knowledge and the beginning of knowledge, but something else is needed: "form," or the understanding of what one perceives in the light of universal essence structures. This does not mean I cannot know individuals; it is just that I have to know them in this intellectual light.

One could put it this way: if I had the choice between losing, say, my literal vision or this power of understanding in the "light" of universal essences, I would without hesitation choose to lose my eyesight. And this is not just me: when I pose this same question to students in my classes over the years, no student—not even one!—has ever chosen for losing intellectual insight and understanding over actual, sensual seeing. Losing one's eyesight is, of course, a horror. But notice, I would still remain fully intact as a functioning person if I lost my eyesight. But if I lost this power to understand in the light of universals, I could still be a person, but I could not function like one anymore.

Not only do persons possess the power of grasping things in their universal nature, insofar as human beings possess a specifically personal intellect, they also possess free will as well. If so, there is here another difference (Chapter 9) between biological causes and conditions from personal freedom. For freedom refers to a unique kind of cause—that of being an uncaused (or first cause)—as opposed to all biological and bio-chemical causes, which are exclusively caused (or secondary) causes.

What difference do the above points make for psychology, whose primary object of study are persons? It is, of course, important to do justice to a person's biological and bio-chemical natures, as well as sense and instinctual natures. But this is only half of the story. Persons are capable of rationally understanding individual things in light of universal essences, and then responding adequately to them with one's will. Rational psychology will be the topic of Chapter 7. But before turning to it, Chapter 6 will consider the empirical nature of psychology.

Locating the Empirical in Psychology

In the last two chapters, various objects of a properly psychological investigation were identified. Practically all the phenomena examined were not empirical in nature: not the conscious self, not psychic acts performed by the self, nor the various kinds of products produced by those psychic acts. None of these psychic phenomena are sensibly or empirically given. One can make inferences from psychic phenomena stemming from empirical data, as this chapter will make evident, but it is not as if empirical data can somehow stand on its own without some reference to non-empirical, psychic experiences. The only remaining possible objects of psychological inquiry were individual and social behavior, learning theory, developmental psychology, as well as the causes and conditions for psychic events. But causes and conditions for psychic events also presuppose…psychic phenomena. Furthermore, behavior and learning theory presuppose non-empirical psychic phenomena; otherwise, no one can distinguish specifically psychological behavior from any other kind of behavior. And without performing inner psychic acts, no one can learn anything.

It seems from these last two chapters that in the battle between the non-empirical and empirical dimensions of psychology, the non-empirical dimension has not only won but has totally vanquished the empirical, which in today's climate is a rather eccentric position. Even if one grants that the empirical dimension of psychology cannot stand alone and on its own, independent of any relations or at least implicit presuppositions going back to non-empirical psychic factors, there still needs to be a place for the empirical in psychology.

It is unnecessary to give some kind of proof for the existence of empirical psychology. Psychology journals and textbooks are full of important empirical studies. Instead, my interest here will be unfolding something of the nature of empirical psychology. Some progress was made in this direction at the end of the last chapter, concerning the kind of intelligibility empirical phenomena possess in whatever empirical science one is investigating, as opposed to properly philosophical objects. Philosophical objects need a more perfect kind of intelligibility to justify intellectual intuition into the universal essence structure itself, whereas empirical objects only have to be meaningful, that is, following intelligible patterns without presupposing any kind of direct insight into the empirical universal.

In this chapter, I want to further explore those aspects of psychological reality empirical psychology sees, and then incorporate and balance that empirical dimension with other psychological perspectives that are seen by the other disciplines and given in our naïve lived experience.

It is helpful to imagine psychological reality as one large circle containing a series of smaller overlapping circles. One of the bigger or at least more developed of the smaller circles concerns empirical psychology. This circle of empirical psychology is not self-contained or independent of the other smaller circles, as these other circles are needed in order to properly grasp and then correctly interpret psychological, empirical phenomena. Again, psychological reality is essentially conscious or oriented toward conscious life. Relations to conscious life can be explicitly denied. But even in these investigations, consciousness still has to be implicitly presupposed. It cannot be absolutely and consistently rejected.

If the above is correct, the other smaller circles are crucially important, not only for understanding the overall large circle of total psychological reality, but also for properly understanding the smaller circle of empirical, psychological phenomena. In this Chapter, I especially want to develop—besides the "place" of empirical psychology within psychology proper—some of the other smaller inner "circles," like the psychological insights coming from literature and theology.

To understand the nature of empirical psychology, consider first the overall method of empirical investigation in general, whether of psychology or biology or physics. Perhaps a good place to begin is to note C. S. Lewis' common sense approach to modern science. He states,

> Science works by experiments. It watches how things behave. Every scientific statement in the long run, however complicated it looks, really means something like, 'I point the telescope to such and such a part of the sky at 2:20 a.m. on January 15th and saw so-and-so,' or, 'I put some of this stuff in a pot and heated it to such-and-such a temperature and it did so-and-so.' Do not think I am saying anything against science: I am only saying what its job is. And the more scientific a man is, the more (I believe) he would agree with me that this is the job of science—and a very useful and necessary job it is too.[96]

Notice how Lewis aligns empirical science closely to observation and experimentation.* The further science gets away from concrete empirical observations and more towards a more theoretical understanding of things, the more philosophical, or at least the more theoretical, it becomes. The natural sciences cannot simply jettison observation of really existing, sensible phenomena entirely, as science would then become only speculation about natural phenomena, or worse, science fiction. What really differentiates scientists from philosophers is the role that empirical observation and experimentation plays, which philosophers may at times presuppose but not do themselves use (unless, of course, they are also scientists).

*THE MATHEMATICAL DIMENSION OF NATURAL SCIENCE

In the above quote, C. S. Lewis neglects the tremendous role that mathematics play in the natural sciences. Perhaps a more sophisticated summary of the methodology of the natural sciences comes from Edward Dougherty, who states,

> Scientific knowledge can be defined in terms of a duality between mathematics (mind) and observation (phenomena). More precisely, it both requires and provides a specifically defined link between mind and phenomena.

> Four conditions must be satisfied to have a valid scientific theory: (1) There is a mathematical model expressing the theory. (2) Precise relationships, known as "operational definitions," are specified between terms in the theory and measurements of corresponding physical events. (3) There is validating data: there is a set of future quantitative predictions derived from the theory and measurements of corresponding physical events. (4) There is a statistical analysis that supports acceptance of the theory, that is, supports the concordance of the predictions with the physical measurements—including the mathematical theory justifying the application of the statistical methods.

> The theory must be expressed in mathematics because science involves relations between measurable quantities, and mathematics concerns such relations. There must also be precise relationships specified between a theory and corresponding observations; otherwise, the theory would not be rigorously connected to physical phenomena. Third, observations must confirm predictions made from the theory. Lastly, owing to randomness, concordance of theory and observation must be characterized statistically.[97]

I mention this role of mathematics to show that the pure natural sciences (biology, chemistry and physics) are also—like with psychology—not totally reducible to empirical or sensible observation and induction. These empirical sciences not only presuppose basic metaphysical principles (non-contradiction, identity, etc.), they also presuppose mathematics. Both metaphysical principles and mathematics in turn require intellectual intuition. Not only is psychology not a "pure" empirical science—in the sense of being independent from metaphysical and mathematical presuppositions— neither are the natural sciences.

I want to further investigate the kind of knowledge generated by the empirical approach, first in general and then as applied to psychology. Notice the actual content of each of the empirical sciences is supplied, not by philosophy, but rather by the actual empirical investigations performed. In general, this method is about using sense observation to understand really existing particulars by discovering general patterns. For example, one can observe one zebra as striped, and then many thousands as striped. From those accumulated observations, we can rightly* infer that it belongs to the general nature of zebras (or zebraness) that "all" are striped. Of course, no one has ever directly observed (or empirically intuited) *all* zebras, so with this assertion, we are concluding more than what is strictly given by all these combined observations. Nor can anyone directly intuit—specifically, with "the eye of the mind"—the universal nature of zebraness to "intellectually see" that it belongs to the inner nature of zebraness to be striped (for the simple reason that no such intuition is given[98]). Thus, our knowledge of this fact is only given from empirical intuitions of individual, really existing zebras, and inductive generalizations from them.* In contrast, everyone can in principle "intellectually see" into the general nature of *responsibility* that—absolutely and in principle—that it *presupposes freedom,* that *the diagonals of a perfect square (on a flat surface) are exactly equal,* and that *love is intrinsically good.*

*THE PRINCIPLE OF INDUCTION

Intellectual intuition not only justifies mathematics and basic metaphysical principles crucial to all science, it even is that the basis of the principle of induction, so central to the empirical method.

What justifies this move from observation of concrete particulars to an understanding of an individual being in the light of its species is the principle of induction. This principle states that from a representative sample of observations of some kind of being or behavior, we can *rightly* conclude that the instances not observed—of that kind of being—will be or behave like the instances observed. For example, the ancient Egyptians noticed that the star Sirius rises from the horizon precisely once every 365 and a quarter days. What is it that justifies their thinking that it will continue to do so in the future? Because this phenomenon has happened every year for thousands of years, one can rightly assume that it will—probably—happen again next year. But why? The answer ultimately is because of the basic intelligibility of the world. Things make sense. The world is not chaos, but a cosmos (an ordered whole), which allows for reasons for things. This presupposition is at the heart of the empirical method.

The principle of induction is itself true via insight (or intellectual intuition). Induction is not itself reducible to or explainable by the empirical method because it (the principle of induction) is itself an essential ingredient of that method, and it is logical nonsense to apply a principle in order to establish it (without begging the question).

Practically all strict empirical argumentation works inductively. For example, one only knows about zebraness (that is, general species characteristics) inductively and indirectly from the accumulated individual, really existing zebras that have in fact been observed. With inductive argumentation, the conclusion is never strictly necessary or absolute, as there could obviously be exceptions with other potential observations of instances not empirically observed. Perhaps albino zebras really do exist. In contrast, those arguments whose conclusions claim *all* the information needed for the truth of a conclusion best lend themselves to a deductive logical approach.*

*TWO BASIC KINDS OF PROOF AND TWO BASIC KINDS OF INTUITION

Every proof (or argument) goes from a premise or premises to a conclusion. Sometimes we can extend our knowledge beyond what can be directly seen by "proving" some conclusion. Every proof works indirectly through evidence presented by premises, as opposed to other instances where no proof is necessary because some assertion is already self-evident (that is, there is now a direct seeing). For example, it is impossible to prove (through something else) that *something cannot both exist and not exist simultaneously.* It is, after all, a "first" principle, which is the basis for all other proofs, but it is itself unprovable. But that doesn't mean it cannot be known, understood and justified. It is actually the clearest of facts, known and explainable as being self-evidently true.

Sometimes the same thesis can be both self-evident and accessible to being proved through something else, such as the thesis that *2+2=4*, (although proof through something else—that is, through evidence—in this instance is unnecessary).

There are two basic kinds of proofs and two basic kinds of direct seeing (or intuition). The two indirect kinds of argument are inductive and deductive proofs, and the two basic kinds of direct seeing are empirical and intellectual intuition.

Here is an example of each kind of proof: First, an example of an inductive argument:

> This zebra is striped
> This second zebra is striped
> <u>This third zebra is striped, etc. (to a representative sample)</u>
> Therefore, all zebras are striped

Now an example of a deductive argument:

> All persons possess the power of intellect
> <u>All intellectual beings must also possess the power of volition</u>
> Therefore, all persons possess the power of volition

Notice that with both these forms of argumentation, a person goes from evidence—as presented by the premises—to a conclusion. In other words, the truth the conclusion establishes goes through premises. If a proof is needed, it suggests that the conclusion standing alone without support is insufficient.

Both these indirect kinds of argumentation can be contrasted to another kind of evidence that is direct (or, in other words, is self-evident), such as our examples from the text that *responsibility presupposes freedom* and that *contradictory theses cannot both be true*. The truth of both of these assertions goes back to intellectual intuition.

Besides intellectual intuition, there is a second kind of direct seeing that goes back to empirical intuition (or sense perception). An example of this kind of intuition is the observation that the earth has one moon and the planet Jupiter has at least 39 moons. The "matter" of all empirical science goes back to empirical intuition and induction (inductive proof). The (subject) "matter" of much of philosophy and mathematics[99] ultimately goes back to intellectual intuition and deductive proof.

Why are all these distinctions important? Remember the discussion in Chapter 1 concerning the importance of reading academic topics in a critical way, whereby having a sense for the kind and degree of evidence for the truth of an assertion was crucial for genuine knowledge versus mere ideology. It is very helpful while reading psychological studies to have an eye on the actual evidence and the kind of evidence a text provides, or does not provide, for its assertions. This evidence can be self-evident, such as *2+2=4*, going back to intellectual intuition. Or this self-evidence can go back to some individual empirical observation, such as *this zebra is striped*. Alternatively, evidence can either be inductive (a conclusion based on a representative sample, *all zebras are striped*) or deductive (such as with geometrical reasoning from first principles).

Finally, perhaps the evidence for assertions goes back only to an inference to the best explanation (see below) or merely to some model that has been generated. Ideally, as noted above, that model should be mathematically based. But often in psychology it is not, such as with B. F. Skinner's claim that "mind" is an "explanatory fiction" or Sigmund Freud's notion of "being conscious" being a "term" (Chapter 4). With all these various methods, there will be differing kinds and degrees of certainty involved.

Scientists are certainly interested in really existing particular instances, but almost exclusively from the point of view of how they can then shed "intellectual light" on their respective species or be instances of some general physical or chemical law. Notice when it comes to biological species, as well as chemical and physical laws, there will be individual variations, say, from one beetle to the next of the same species. There could even be exceptions. But even when there are such differences, they typically, in turn, reveal other sub-distinctions within a species, which in turn can be universalized.

Furthermore, to use this or that individual beetle merely as a representative instance of a species (that is, as a specimen) obviously implies no disrespect to that beetle. There is, of course, a dimension of that beetle that is unique to it as an individual—such as its real, individual existence—but scientists are far less interested in what is unique to that beetle as to what is common to all the beetles of that species. And by unfolding what is common to that species, biologists can then obtain a far better understanding of this individual beetle, as well as (of course) all the other individual beetles of that species.

Empirical psychology runs the same way. It typically has a different content than biology or chemistry—insofar as its central focus is conscious life—but it too is interested in observing really existing particular objects and events to get at some kind of species knowledge or universal principle. The central focus here, as with the other natural sciences and with philosophy, is on the universal. All of science and philosophy want, in the end, an elucidation of a universal knowledge of individual things. It is, for instance, less interested in this particular insect as it is with this kind of insect, its species. Then from that universal understanding, one can come back and have a much better perspective and understanding of the individual, seeing the individual "in the (intellectual) light" of its universal.

One central question is this: how can the empirical method work when its primary datum, consciousness, is not empirically given? Our inner conscious life, with its psychic acts together with the personal self that performs them, is not sensibly given.[100] For, after all, no psychic phenomena (that is, psychic being, psychic acts or products of those acts) are so many inches high or long, is colored or gaseous, etc. How then can this method work on these phenomena?

It seems to me any psychology that *exclusively* touts the empirical method cannot in any kind of theoretically adequate way do justice to psychological phenomena and methodology. They end up quietly presupposing psychological realities such as conscious phenomena that they simply cannot empirically justify, or worse, pretend that such phenomena are scientifically irrelevant or even non-existent.[101] To give any kind of explanation of psychological realities, there has to be some implicit presupposition of or reference to inner psychic phenomena. The empirical method, however, can work if this presupposition is made, and then it is possible to investigate conscious phenomena in an inductive way, as well as using inference to best explanation.*

*INFERENCE TO BEST EXPLANATION

Earlier in Chapter 4, I mentioned that the notion of inference to best explanation[102] was widely used in both natural science and philosophy. The reason for this use is because both intuition (empirical and/or intellectual) and strict inferences from them (proof) are sometimes not clearly enough given, and thinkers have to resort more to theories and hypotheses the explain phenomena. This is also what psychologists will typically do as well. Thus, psychologists will almost universally claim to be strict empiricists, and yet they will invariably talk about blatantly non-empirical phenomena. Thus, Freud will talk about repression,

Karen Horney's anxiety, Carl Rogers's self-actualization, and Carl Jung's psychological archetypes. Not one of these topics are empirical in nature, nor are there easy inferences to them from empirical data. They are, at best, scientific models (although hardly mathematical models) to describe phenomena. Still, there is some justification to speak of them in this more theoretical way (despite a resulting tension between their stated method and actual practice).

There is a real difference in the kind of certainty one has from intuition—whether empirical or intellectual—as opposed to some theory coming from inferences to best explanation. For example, while I might have a reasonable and satisfying theory concerning repression and anxiety that explains well all the pieces of evidence and symptoms one finds empirically, I do *not* have a theory that I am now working at my desk because I know and directly experience it. Similarly, I do *not* have a theory that 2+2=4, I (intellectually) see it.

There is nothing wrong with inferences to best explanation, if neither intuitive nor deductive approaches are possible. The limits of this approach, however, need to be respected. One ought not to forget that this method is more speculative, and thus less certain. One should especially not deny what is more evident for the sake of that which is less evident, that is, philosophical insights for the sake of some theory, such as Freud ignoring or denying evident insights into the natural moral law by explaining all morality in terms of sublimation.

Now I want to turn to three illustrations of how an application of the empirical method to non-empirical psychic phenomena can be accomplished.

First, take the phenomena of mental illness, where a person's approach toward reality is somehow maladaptive, skewed (in neurosis) or even broken (in psychosis). Let us suppose someone beginning to study this phenomenon in concrete, lived experience will eventually come to notice, from across a broad spectrum of instances, reoccurring patterns of behavior and inner psychological experiences. These patterns will crystalize into various kinds of psychological syndromes that can be identified, named and empirically investigated. Then when psychologists do their therapy, they will notice clients showing symptoms that fall into one or another of these general categories that have been already identified and named, such as obsessive-compulsive behavior or bipolar disorders. With the understanding that comes from prior empirical research into the different kinds of syndromes, psychologists will then have a clearer understanding of their own clients' particular psychological disorder, just as a biologist can understand this individual beetle far more clearly by understanding its general species. Of course, there is always the danger of miscategorization in psychology. That danger, however, is just as possible with other biological or medical issues, as well as with all the other sciences.

Second, let us say someone is having issues with depression or anxiety. It does not make any sense to deny the reality of these psychic events just because they are not empirically observable. And yet, even if psychic phenomena are not directly empirically observable, empirical science could still have something to say about them. Perhaps psychologists—from the self-report of their clients—have observed that some kinds of medications will help alleviate such feelings, or perhaps there are certain behavioral techniques that have worked with similar cases to counter similar instances of depression and anxiety.

One of the very first issues that typically comes up, whether explicitly or implicitly, in psychological treatment is whether the primary source of some psychological dysfunction is bio-chemically caused or intentionally motivated by some object. For example, imagine the case of someone who in his or her interpersonal relationship with others is doing well. This person seems well-adjusted, having rewarding relationships with others and has discovered meaning in his life. And yet...he is still racked with serious anxiety and depression issues. With this kind of case, it seems reasonable to strongly suspect that the main issue is something biochemical in nature.

In contrast, suppose another person is similarly racked with anxiety and depression issues, and upon further psychological investigation, it turns out this person feels terribly alone. Imagine that his girlfriend, his only friend in the world, has left him, and in his utter loneliness, he is having a crisis of meaning and of self-worth. In this case, while some kind of drug therapy might still in some way be necessary, there seems little doubt that the primary focus should be on therapy that could assist this person in helping him discover meaning and self-worth, as well as perhaps help with interpersonal relations.

Here, as well as with the above other cases, the therapist could be helped by knowing what clinically has worked with other similar cases from psychological literature: investigating the kind of drug therapy that has worked in the past with people having this patient's symptoms, or applying Victor Frankl's logotherapy or Martin Seligman's positive psychology to those having a crisis of meaning. Professional psychologists do not work in a void. They have expertise as to what has worked in the past with other similar cases, and in that way, apply the empirical method. Thus, even here, concerning his inner conscious life, there is an understanding of an individual psychological syndrome in the light of these other similar cases, and then adapting a specific therapeutic procedure that has shown success from those other instances.

Finally, consider learning theory, such as the work of Jean Piaget (1896-1980). Piaget observed small children, including infants, to try to understand their inner, primitive psychological experience. This was done by directly intuiting psychic states via bodily expression, by empathetically feeling what they might be going through, and by making theoretical inferences to best explanation concerning the inner experience of their infantile conscious life. Then from all these sources and methods, he was able to generalize his discoveries by distinguishing various stages he thought all human infants and children pass through. Even though their own inner conscious life was beyond his direct reach, as they were too young even to give a self-report, he was still able to articulate something of their inner conscious experience.

Notice with all three above examples of empirical psychological research, there is no serious or consistent application of any kind of (total) psychological empiri*cism*, whereby non-empirical psychic states are considered simply irrelevant or thought of as not existing. On the contrary, this semi-empirical approach has to work in tandem—at least implicitly—with trying to understand the reality of inner, conscious states of others.

If inner psychic states are not given empirically, how are they then given? First and foremost, they are given to our own individual, personal conscious life from within. Such experiences are neither empirical in nature (via sense perception) nor are they directly accessible scientifically via observation, as they exclusively go back to a private, inner and non-empirical dimension of each person's own naïve lived experience. Secondly, with respect to the psychic experiences of others, they can be given through the medium of their bodily expression.

One philosopher who misses the phenomenon of bodily expression is Rene Descartes (1596-1650), whose philosophy was captured by Gilbert Ryle's famous expression that living bodies are nothing but "ghosts (the soul) in a machine (the body),"[103] that is, as if the experience of one's own and other bodies are nothing but lifeless matter extended in space. This way of viewing our bodies makes the body-soul dimensions of our human nature too separate from each other, so separated that that body is not expressive of soul.

This Cartesian view is not really anyone's concrete, non-theoretical experience of others. A normal way of perceiving other human bodies is not that of lifeless matter but as expressive of their own inner, psychological life. All of us can sometimes directly "see" or intuit the joy or sorrow of others, their hope or their despair *as expressed through* their face and especially their eyes. We experience other persons as body/soul unities formed into one being and not in some radical dualistic way as un-unified bodies and souls.*

*TWO FORMS OF DUALISM

Some kind of dualism has to be maintained by anyone who is not a sheer materialist. There is, however, another far less innocent form of dualism. I will here distinguish both forms.

The first recognizes a relative distinction of body and soul in human beings, which is not eviscerated by their forming the unity of one human person. This kind of unity is, therefore, different from a unity of fusion, such as when two pieces of steel are fused into one, losing their individual identities in the larger piece of steel. In contrast to this unity of fusion, with the dualism found in body and soul, a real unity is established as the soul forms the matter of the body into one human being, but without a complete loss of the distinction between body and soul. Thus, the interiority of the conscious self remains as relatively distinct from a person's body. What follows is that the (material) body can be expressive of (the immaterial) soul as the soul is immersed in the body, forming an intimate unity of body and soul.

There is, however, a second form of dualism, which is sometimes called radical dualism, where the distinction between body and soul is so emphasized that they do not enter into a unity. Instead of the soul being immersed in the body, where it could then be expressive of soul, Descartes thinks that the body-soul relation is side-by-side. The only real connection between them is via causality, such as with fear causing bodily reactions and bio-chemistry causing depression. An even more extreme form of radical dualism comes from Plato, who thinks of the body as not even part of our human nature, as it is merely a "prison-house" of the soul.

This text began with a critique of empiricism, that is, where the only acceptable psychological method is empirical because the only kind of fact is empirical facts. While the empirical method is one legitimate avenue to psychological truth, this method cannot work alone and requires other approaches discussed in this text, such as reference to inner conscious experience, empathy, bodily expression, inference to best explanation, as well as the approach of the common sense person, who often experiences what can then be further elaborated philosophically. Now, this chapter will conclude by briefly discussing two further avenues of psychological investigation, again going beyond both empirical and philosophical investigations alone: literature and theology.

Both literature and philosophy are interested in universal truths. Philosophy studies (besides the theme of real existence, that is, of the self, the world and of God) the *abstract universal,* that is, what is universally true about its objects, concerning, for example, the general nature of justice or responsibility or the person. Thus, for example, philosophy is not specifically interested in whether this man has been just to another in some particular situation, but rather what justice is, universally and in principle. Literature is also interested in the universal, but a different kind from that studied by philosophy. Whereas philosophy is primarily interested in the universal as universal (the abstract universal), literature is interested in the *concrete universal,* the universal as illustrated by a particular story.[104] For example, if you want to find out what makes for a good or bad marriage, consider reading something like the philosophical work *Love and Responsibility* by Karol Wojtyla (the late John Paul II). Alternatively, consider reading the novel *Pride and Prejudice* by Jane Austen. Both explain the nature of marriage, both good marriages and bad marriages, but in different ways.

Similar to philosophy, there are all kinds of psychological truths one can find in literature. For example, if you want to find out about the "inner side" of mental illness, that is, what a person suffering from a mental illness is subjectively going through, consider reading *Crime and Punishment,* by the great Russian novelist Fyodor Dostoyevsky (1821-1881). While philosophy needs to make truths *evident* (as opposed to merely stating unsupported assertions), literature wants to *show* these truths as played out concretely in the individual lives of its characters. Not only that, but the novelist can help us get "into the minds," so to speak, of his or her characters, thereby helping us to understand them from the inside. For, after all, it is probably not such a stretch to suppose that literary geniuses have a better concrete understanding of other people than many or most professional psychologists. We can all learn from them.

Turning to empirical psychology, including all of the natural sciences, it was already noted how the natural sciences are interested in universal truths via the application of the principle of induction from observations of concrete particular instances. This approach works especially well with the objects that biology, physics and chemistry investigate, where the individual, as an individual, is almost completely understood in the light of the generic (or universal). In other words, the individual differences between this beetle and that beetle of the same species are not really so great, and practically everything you need to know about this beetle is contained in a generic understanding of *beetleness.*

When it comes to persons, however, individuality matters, and with each individual person there is a very large dimension that is utterly unique to this person going far beyond the generic, that is, beyond what is common to all human beings. Each one of us is so new that it almost makes sense to say that each person is a new species unto ourselves. One philosopher put it this way: that *human nature has to be redefined after Socrates.*[105] In other words, Socrates is so different, so new and unique to all the other human beings that have gone before him that now human nature itself has to be re-understood all over again. Something similar can be said about each one of us, especially if we live up to our calling *as individuals*, instead of non-thinking drones open to being manipulated and eager to follow the crowd. Each one of us is individually so different in our being, so new in relation to our species. Each one of us is new in a way that anyone insect or plant is not in relation to their respective species.

Thus, empirical methodology works especially well with non-personal phenomena because the differences from individual to individual within a species are not so great. But when it comes to persons, it is not perfect because individual differences within the species of our common human nature are far larger and highly significant. For example, imagine a man falling in love with a woman. Notice, he does not merely love some generic and interchangeable "woman," he rather loves "this woman." To a real lover, some other woman just will not do. Let us say that after a happy marriage, that woman dies. The experience of the husband is that there is now a hole in being itself, analogous to the extinction of a whole animal species. Whereas, in contrast, if an insect dies, there is obviously nothing analogous, as "this" insect is pretty much like any other instantiation of its species.

My point is this: not only is there a generic dimension with each one of us— what we have in common with every other human being—there also exists with persons a unique, individual dimension that only *this person* possesses. And this individual dimension has its own significance, which the lover especially sees.

As important and successful as empirical methodology is for studying the human beings and the natural world, it is not ideally suited for the study of persons, insofar as the central focus of the natural sciences is to achieve a species understanding by applying the principle of induction to empirically given individuals. Thus, not only is there not a co-extensive identity between empirical facts and facts (as inner, subjective experience and value facts also exist), there is also not a perfect co-extensive identity between empirical psychology and our individual nature as persons, as empirical psychology focuses upon that dimension of human nature that is generalizable, not taking into account its important individual dimension.

What is the discipline that investigates the individual *as individual?* It is great literature. Literature—as opposed to romance novels and Hallmark movies, which are formulaic and thus too generic—will help us understand universal truths, but always within the context of telling a very concrete story. Abstractions are for philosophers; literature is for those especially interested in concrete stories about individual persons. And insofar as these stories are "true," they will adequately exemplify philosophical truths that are pursued more abstractly, which is why reading *Love and Responsibility* and *Pride and Prejudice* together is beneficial. They will be saying the same things in two very different ways.

Now I want to turn a few relations between psychology and theology,* considering briefly three psychological aspects of theology with respect to Christian theology.[106]

*REDUCING THEOLOGY TO PSYCHOLOGY (AND VICE VERSA)

There is a sense in which a certain kind of theology (or religion) can be explained psychologically, such as with idolatry, whereby some contingent (or finite) thing is treated as an absolute. There are good psychological reasons for why one kind of object is absolutized, and not others. For example, if someone suffers from greed by absolutizing money, it makes perfect psychological sense for that person (or group) to formally worship something like the famous Golden Calf, such as during the time of Moses.

This, however, does not justify treating all religion and theology as reducible to psychology, as when theology studies the true absolute. What explains this kind of theology is the Absolute itself and not some subjective psychological projection.

Sometimes, however, there have been attempts to go in the opposite direction, that is, for theology to swallow up psychology. Just as some people within a strict Calvinist tradition will try to reduce a philosophical ethics to theology, so will they at times try to find exclusively biblical answers to psychological questions. Their idea is that since original sin has destroyed human rational powers of intellect and will, a person's only sure recourse is to the bible alone. Thus, in psychology, all one can only appeal to are Bible passages as a source for psychological insight and help.

In contrast to these two extremes, Paul Vitz gives one example of how theology and psychology can work together. It is both good theology and good psychology for people to forgive their enemies. Yet if a person living in a Christian milieu has difficulties forgiving (from long-standing anger and hatred), he or she could easily feel pressured by other

Christians to do what they are not psychologically ready to do: forgive. It belongs to the skill of the therapist to recognize what a client can and cannot do at a particular time. Thus Vitz states,

> The patient does not have full freedom to stop hating, as it can be extremely difficult to abandon hate-filled structures built up over many years. But people do have the freedom to begin to stop hating...to let go of hatreds—and to maintain that focus over time, since it is common that the choice to let go of hatred has to be made many times and with respect to different memories and interpretations of the enemy.

The work of the psychologist is to understand the psychological basis for "hate-filled structures" that can dominate certain personalities, and for the therapist to see the crucial importance of forgiveness, as well as to have a sense for the many psychological steps it takes for a person to give up these long-established patterns. Theology can be one source of good psychology, such as the need to forgive. But the bible can no more give advice as to how and when this can be fruitfully accomplished within a therapeutic setting than it can explain biology or chemistry.[107]

First, in orthodox Christianity, the belief is that Christ is both fully God and fully human (establishing the truth or falsity of this assertion is not here my business). As the divine nature of Christ is believed to be perfect, it follows that Christ's humanity also has to be perfect. If so, Christ is then the one who teaches us how to be human. One facet of psychology is the study of what it means to be human, that is, fully fulfilled and flourishing.

Secondly, Paul Vitz, in his work *Psychology as Religion*, investigates the Christian roots of humanistic psychology. He claims that the thought of people like Carl Rogers and Abraham Maslow did not arise spontaneously, insofar as "the first popular expression of such notions as 'self-realization,' 'becoming a real person,' and the like appears to have occurred in New York's Protestant pulpits."[108] They were rather a continuation of certain Christian ideas from authors of the 19th century, specifically Harry Emerson Fosdick and Norman Vincent Peale, who emphasized many of the same themes as do these humanists. In the following quote, Vitz quotes Fosdick,

> What is Christianity? 'The divine origin, spiritual nature, infinite worth, and endless possibilities' of each 'personality,' he [Fosdick] tells us, with its 'power of intellect, creative hope and love,' and 'promise of development' constitute the 'essential genius' of Christianity. That is, the individual personality with all its promise for creative development

is the central Christian concept. Given Fosdick's emphasis on the two ideas of progress and personality, one is hardly surprised that this line of thinking evolved by 1943 into a theoretical position much like today's selfism. Even the title of Fosdick's third and extremely popular book, *On Being a Real Person*, brings to mind the current situation, for Rogers entitled his most popular work *On Becoming a Person* (1961).[109]

I do not find anything particularly amiss with this debt of humanistic psychology to liberal Protestant thought, especially since it shows in yet another way the intersection between psychology and theology. It helps, furthermore, to expose as problematic the impression that psychology likes to foster of simply being dependent upon empirical, psychological research as its only guide. Not only is psychology dependent upon philosophy, it is also dependent (at least for inspiration) upon certain theological considerations, such as with Vitz's example of the Protestant ideas of "self-realization" and "becoming a real person," which become central ideas within humanistic psychology.

There are psychological dimensions which empirical psychology is less suited to study: not only inner, conscious states that are simply excluded from all direct empirical investigation, but also the individual *as individual* and the individual *as fully fulfilled and flourishing*. Empirical psychology, in contrast, is far better suited to study the individual from the point of view as a member of a species and as factually given, as opposed to what ought to be, to what is proper and fitting to our human nature.

Finally (third), one can apply a broad distinction between *being* and *thinking* specifically to the difference between authentic morality and virtue signaling. While moral values refer to the way some persons *exist*—in the sense that certain persons really are in their character morally good—virtue signaling, in contrast, is a mere product of thinking and posturing. There is an obvious difference between someone merely thinking or pretending to be morally good from others who (in their character) really are morally good. Virtue signaling (together with moral hypocrisy and moral value blindness) really are psychological constructs, and as such, are of primary interest to the discipline of psychology. Moral character, in contrast, is not reducible to a psychological construct, but rather is a mode of being. Thus, a clear distinction needs to be made between both sets of phenomena.

Furthermore, not only is virtue signaling and moral hypocrisy not indicative of the presence of moral value, they are also actually contrary to authentic morality. There is, in fact, an inverse relationship between them, such that the greater the presence of virtue signaling, the less authentic moral goodness. Conversely, the greater the moral goodness, the less virtue signaling.

How does this apply to theology? Consider the following two quotes from the Christian scriptures, first concerning virtue signaling and the second about value blindness.

> Take care not to perform righteous deeds in order that people may see them; otherwise, you will have no recompense from your heavenly Father. When you give alms, do not blow a trumpet before you, as the hypocrites do in the synagogues and in the streets to win the praise of others. Amen, I say to you, they have received their reward. But when you give alms, do not let your left hand know what your right is doing, so that your almsgiving may be secret.[110]

> Why do you notice the splinter in your brother's eye, but do not perceive the wooden beam in your eye? You hypocrite, remove the wooden beam from your eye first; then you will see clearly to remove the splinter from your brother's eye.[111]

One hardly needs to be a Christian believer to see the truth of the above passages. What it shows—among many other possible examples—is how theological, philosophical and psychological truth are not completely different, independent spheres. Psychology does not and should not stand alone, exclusively dependent upon empirical observation and research. Rather, psychology limits and is delimited by other philosophical, literary and even theological considerations. Why? Because ultimately, truth is one, which can be brought out and investigated from all these differing perspectives.

Despite the obvious success and appropriateness of a strictly empirical approach to psychology, it should not overlook other legitimate, and sometimes decisively important, avenues of psychological insight. In the next three chapters, I want to investigate yet another extremely important avenue of psychology, going well beyond empirical psychology: the investigation of human beings specifically *as persons*. It is difficult for empirical psychology to even identify, much less do justice to, the personal nature of our being.

Chapter 7

Human Nature and Rational Psychology

This chapter will investigate the relationship between human nature—its generic and, specifically, its rational dimension—and the discipline of psychology, as the first (human nature) determines or should determine the second (psychology). This is especially important concerning our rational nature, insofar as this dimension is what makes us not merely highly ordered animals, but persons. Despite this crucial importance, it seems to me that mainline psychology barely notices our distinctively rational and therefore personal nature. If it did, one would expect whole chapters on the rational powers of intellect and will in introductory psychology texts. Such chapters are, unfortunately, completely missing in these texts.

Then, in the second half of this chapter, a reflection will be given as to how this rational nature can be theoretically helpful for the discipline of psychology. Historically, before the turn to empirical psychology in the late 19th century, psychology was enfolded into philosophy and called *rational psychology*. While psychology, in general, is obviously not reducible to rational psychology, insofar as empirical psychology also exists, it is also not nothing either.[112] And, as discussed throughout this text, both empirical and philosophical insights need to be integrated together for a more complete understanding of psychology.

Before turning to rational psychology, some reflection needs to be given as to what it means to possess a personal, rational nature because it is only by first understanding our personal nature that any investigation into rational psychology makes sense. Then in the following two chapters, I want to investigate the psychological reality and significance of the classical two central powers of a specifically rational soul: intellect and will.

What is meant by the term *rationality*? This notion is closely associated with an earlier idea of *intelligibility*. In Chapter 5, it was noted how intelligibility refers to the inner meaningfulness of things, and therefore their knowability. Things make sense, which is a necessary condition for the possibility of science. B. F. Skinner recognizes this point when he states, "Science is … a search for order, for uniformities, for lawful relations among events in nature. It begins, as we all begin, by observing single episodes, but it quickly passes on to the general rule, to scientific law."[113]

Consider the opposite: reality is just haphazard and chaotic, not only without any discernable patterns, but without any patterns whatsoever. For example, let us say every time you measure the boiling point of water at sea level, you get a wildly different reading. Then imagine these differences not going back to other different, individual conditions that could in turn be intelligibly identified within their own general pattern. Rather, there is no pattern present at all. Now imagine this same chaotic variability applying not only to the boiling of water but to everything else as well. It is obvious such a scenario is the death knell for science.[114]

This notion of intelligibility is closely associated with rationality, insofar as those powers which allow for a being to both intellectually grasp and then adequately respond—both volitionally (with one's will) and affectively (from one's heart)—to that intelligibility is what is meant by rationality. A being is rational if it can grasp and then adequately respond to the real existence and inner meaningfulness of things, especially in the intellectual "light" of their universal essences.* It is, therefore, the relation between this inherent intelligibility yielding meaningful patterns on the one hand with the intellectual, volitional and affective powers to grasp and then adequately respond to them on the other, which constitutes rationality. Everything that is possesses intelligibility is in principle knowable. But only some beings—rational beings—can grasp this intelligibility. Thus rationality, which is a topic specifically within the philosophy of the person, is different from intelligibility, a topic within general metaphysics.

*THE TWO BASIC KINDS OF UNIVERSAL ESSENCES

It is important to keep in mind that rationality goes back to an understanding of and right response to the basic intelligibility of things, and this intelligibility is especially brought out by understanding individual things via their universal. This universal can then, in turn, be identified as going back to either empirical or intellectual intuition. Empirical intuition is only of really existing particulars, and they thereby require inductive generalization to reach their respective universal. This universal is not itself given, as it is only the result of an inductive inference. In contrast, intellectual intuition refers to a direct insight into the universal essence as such.

Both kinds of intuition—either indirect (via the empirical particular) or direct (via an intellectual "seeing" of the universal as such)—reach two very different kinds of universal. And both approaches are uniquely personal in nature. Animals can no more do science as they can do mathematics or philosophy because they cannot understand reality in the light of universals.

Human beings also possess other powers that are not rational. While instincts and our biological senses can be used intelligently by persons possessing rational powers, these kinds of powers are not themselves rational as they can also be found in non-rational, lower animals.[115] Sense powers and instincts are intelligible as they can be known, understood and rationally used. But they are not themselves rational, insofar as they cannot understand nor respond to intelligible patterns within reality—whether empirical or philosophical— without (specifically personal) rational powers. If a being possesses rational powers of intellect and will, such a being will also be personal in nature. It is the possession of rational powers that identifies a being as a person.

What is the connection between rationality and psychology? Earlier in Chapter 2, two levels of authenticity were distinguished: the first concerned only being true to one's own feelings and thinking. This is a more immanent activity (that is, only circling around the self without a transcendent reference to reality), and it is also one that psychologists and philosophers (such as Carl Rogers and Jean Paul Sartre) often equate with someone being authentic. This bar, while real, seems rather low. For, after all, a psychopath could very well know his own mind and yet is hardly fulfilled in any serious sense.

The second level of authenticity refers not only to being true to one's self, but also being true to those insights and truths that have been vouchsafed (or granted) to us over our life. This second level references precisely our rational nature and measures ourselves according to some transcendent standard. Its operation is thereby not immanent or self-enclosed. Instead of a person measuring reality merely according to his or her own subjective needs and instincts—the "buffered self," as Charles Taylor[116] puts it—intelligible reality rather measures the individual according to some rational standard, such as the standards of truth and goodness.

However, the mere presence of a rational power does not guarantee the proper application of it, just as (analogously) the mere presence of a clock does not mean it can accurately tell time. Thus, a person can put his or her rational powers not only to the service of truth and goodness, but also for the end of pleasure and power.* The mere presence of the power of rationality does not imply any fulfillment of its nature, such as when someone possessing a rational nature can still be carried away by some irrational passion. In contrast to persons, insofar as animals are in the fully personal sense non-rational beings, since they cannot understand reality (Chapter 5), they cannot act irrationally.[117]

*FIRST NATURE, SECOND NATURE AND SELF-DETERMINATION

Philosophers within the Aristotelian and Thomistic traditions make a helpful distinction between first and second nature. Our first nature goes back to the basic (ontological) givenness of the kind of being we possess. We are beings possessing instincts and sense perception, together with a rational or personal nature: of intellect and will. In contrast, our second nature refers to the kind of being we become on the basis of how we freely use our first nature. Thus, as persons, we have the power of self-determination, which refers exclusively to our second nature. It clearly does not refer to our first nature, which comes as a given, perhaps even as a gift.

One philosopher, Jean Paul Sartre (1905-1980), denies that things have inherent natures.[118] He thereby conflates first and second natures, reducing the first into the second. This radicalizes personal freedom, making it total, as if all meaning goes back to our arbitrary freedom. He refuses the notion of gift (including our ontological being and nature— our first nature—which is given to us) and wants to make everything a product of our own work. Thus, his thought goes in the direction of idealism (Chapter 1) and towards Marxism.

Pure animals, too, can achieve relations to reality. Animals are not like rocks, which exist in an environment but—outside of being links in a causal chain— cannot establish relations to it. While animals can come in contact with reality through their perception and instincts, they still lack the inwardness to grasp *that* they are perceiving something, that is, the power to grasp facts.

One can get an intuitive glimpse of this last point by considering the strange experience of locking eyes with a cow. The cow seems to be simultaneously seeing you and, oddly, in another sense, not seeing you. It obviously sees you insofar as it has eyes and can react to your sudden movements. But in another sense, it does not seem to be seeing you at all, as it has "vacant eyes." It seems to lack the inwardness to *register* the fact *that* it is seeing you, which involves lateral self-presence. In other words, the conscious life of a pure animal lacks an inward presence to itself, an insufficiency—perhaps even total insufficiency—of an inner, conscious life, that is, of self-possession.[119] An inner, conscious life requires not only intentionality—an "object orientation" that is essentially conscious—but also self-presence. Of course, animals can perceive; they just lack the inwardness to perceive facts, that is, to know reflexively—by taking a slight "step back" and realizing—*that something is* or *is not*. Thus, the full transcendence that personal beings are able to achieve in relation to the world—to know things-in-themselves as well as facts about them—is simply missing. They only perceive beings only from their own point of view, insofar as they can fulfill their own needs and instincts, and not from the point of view of the thing itself, much less from the point of view of a universal understanding of the nature of that thing.

This is not to say that some higher-order animals do not also possess a certain kind of animal rationality, as noted in Chapter 5. This non-personal kind of rationality, however, does not amount to anything like a full transcendence of understanding and responding to another being as it is in-itself (or as it is important-in-itself) or in the light of its universal, which are only granted to persons.

Rationality, in this full sense of knowing and responding adequately to things as they are in-themselves, is not only a mark of personal being; it is the most significant and important characteristic of their nature and fulfillment. Rationality rightly belongs to our "higher nature," and any kind of frustration of that nature will lead a person not only to fail to act in this fully personal way, but also to fail at becoming what persons are meant to become: to be in a right relation to reality, and especially the highest realities.

Consider, in contrast, how it is possible for a person to come to possess great power, fame and wealth, and yet fail to exercise one's own rational nature by knowing what is true and willing what is authentically good. Such a person will be crippled and ultimately frustrated as a person.

If the above reflection on rationality is correct, it means that there is no adequate evaluation of "self-fulfillment" merely by immanent, purely psychological categories. There also needs to be discussion of it via transcendent and relational norms, that is, from the point of view of a person *in relation to reality.* Any psychological self-improvement program that blithely prescinds from such questions will inevitably be marked by superficiality.

Thus, just because human beings possess the power (first nature) to know and respond adequately to things as they are in themselves does not mean that we actually use it (second nature). Yet, despite this obvious truth, human beings are persons, not merely higher-order animals. Not only are we "hardwired" for truth and value—as opposed to pure animals—we will be ultimately frustrated without them. As Aristotle puts it, man is the best of all animals with (the intrinsic value of) justice, but the worst of all animals without (knowing and applying) it.[120]

So far, the focus has been on two variants of rationality—personal and animal—from the point of view of knowledge. Now I want to investigate this same distinction between persons and animals on the volitional side, so as to better identify the kind of rationality human beings possess. There are two kinds[121] of voluntariness—personal and animal—insofar as for both the principle of action lies within their being.

However, before turning to an analysis of their nature and relation, it will be helpful to first distinguish animal volition from mere material causality. Purely material beings (without any life principle) behave by being passively affected externally "from without," as one thing causally impinges upon another thing, inevitably forming a continuous ongoing sequence of causes and effects. Philosophers call this secondary causality, referring to "caused causes." For example, consider the passive activity of a baseball. A baseball is thrown by a pitcher, whose trajectory gets changed when hit by a bat, then landing in the mitt of the fielder. Then that ball is thrown back into the infield. All these changes passively happen to the ball "from without," as opposed to being initiated "from within" by the ball itself.

In contrast to secondary causality, with animal voluntariness the principle of an action lies not outside, but within the being itself. Thus a rabbit, being hunted by a coyote, uses its evasive tactics by scurrying about, seemingly changing direction every ten feet and on a dime. Every change comes from the rabbit, making it far more unpredictable than mere external and passive, secondary causation of something like a baseball. The rabbit is, so to speak, the principle of its own action. However, while the action of a pure animal is voluntary—in the sense that the principle of its action can lie within its being— it is also *determined* from within by its needs and instincts.

In contrast to pure animals, a person is free to either follow the course of his or her instincts or not. A person is able to go against his instinct, say, for self-preservation and risk his life out of love and for the sake of another person. An animal is able to risk its life for the sake of its family—animal or human—but only out of instinct (specifically, the preservation of the species instinct[122]) and not as a response to the threatened beings' intrinsic preciousness, insofar as pure animals cannot even perceive values. It follows that a person is capable of being a "first or uncaused cause," neither determined "from without" from outside material beings nor "from within" from instincts.

It is possible to possess an intellect but (freely) not exercise it. In fact, it is possible for someone to explicitly glory in consciously going against right reason. Thus, one can rightly argue against someone like Plato, who thought that if persons—with perfect knowledge—had a choice between a higher and a lower objective good, they would always choose the higher objective good. Why? Because persons are rational beings, and it is irrational to choose (again assuming sufficient knowledge) a lower objective good over a higher objective one. Thus, for Plato, intellect swallows up the will. In contrast to this intellectual*ism* and rational*ism* of Plato, everyone knows of the experience of seeing something good or true and yet choosing against it for the sake of our lower pleasures. Thus, there are psychological/moral disorders that go back to and are the fruits of our own free decisions, such as from basic immoral attitudes and actions that lead to the growth of passions that can overwhelm the soul.

There are dimensions of a person's *psyche* that can be traced directly back to our own choice and will, such as when we choose something that is morally disordered. Sometimes our own disordered choices will lead to unwilled "fruits," such as depression and anxiety (here, I am referring to that kind of depression and anxiety which is spiritually motivated as opposed to being biochemically caused). Even though these negative psychological "fruits" often come from our free choices, they can also become totally unhinged from our freedom and even come to dominate us as they will take on a certain psychic life of their own. We should be in charge of our own soul, and yet we are sometimes strangely not. "I was no longer captain of my own soul,"[123] as Oscar Wilde puts it, with respect to the ugly fruits of his own passions overwhelming his right reason, leading him to an inner slavery and towards his own self-destruction.

There are other dimensions of our life that are not psychological "fruits" from freely chosen attitudes. They are completely independent of our choice and will, such as with conscious manifestations arising from biochemical causes and genetics. And, of course, there exist disordered patterns coming from one's social environment developed from early childhood. As such, no one (of course) is responsible for their having these kinds of psychological disorders.

The last part of this chapter concerns rational psychology and the two central powers of the soul that are the main theme of rational psychology: intellect and will. Rational or philosophical psychology is actually a vast field—going far beyond contemporary psychology's claim of a simple co-extensive identification of psychology with empirical psychology—grounded in a philosophy of the human person, and covering such topics as emotion, learning, memory, habit, and language. All these topics, while open to having an appropriate empirical dimension, can also be approached from a rational, psychological point of view. For, after all, psychology did not just spring out of thin air from the late nineteenth century but arose from philosophical discussions long before the advent of empirical psychology. This dimension of philosophy was called rational psychology.

The central, governing idea (interpretive key) of rational psychology is this: *that (transcendent) reality serves as the measure of psychological life, and not vice versa.** Thus, the order and rationality of the *psyche* need to mirror the order and intelligibility of reality. When the personal self does not mirror this order, it will then inevitably become disordered and fragmented as a personality.

*IS THE PERSON THE MEASURE OF REALITY OR IS REALITY THE
MEASURE OF THE PERSON?

One central existential question all of us answer in our life, whether
explicitly or implicitly, concerns whether an individual (or more
generally as a culture) is the ultimate source of all meaning, or is there
some pre-given meaning that we need to discover and then live by?

Jean Paul Sartre famously maintains that existence precedes essence, by
which he means that all meaning has to be superimposed by us onto
reality. What constitutes authenticity for Sartre is that this meaning
should be your own and not someone else's. To adopt someone's else
meaning is for Sartre to be inauthentic. The result of this philosophy is
an inevitable conflict between persons, for we are all competing to get
our own meaning adopted or accepted by others and so by the culture.

But what if, besides individual and culturally created meanings
(idealism), there also exists a pre-given meaning that is actually part, so
to speak, of the objective furniture of the world? What if there exists an
inherent meaning or intelligibility that is grounded in reality (realism)
as it is in itself? And what if that kind of meaning is crucial for the
psychological happiness or misery of persons?

Recall again the two meanings (or levels) of authenticity. The first refers
to our being true to our own thinking and willing. This seems to be the
meaning of authenticity that Sartre defends. Yet, it is only the beginning,
as there is a second meaning that refers to being in a right relation to
reality: to what is actually true and authentically good. Consider, for
example, the claim that *Love and justice are intrinsically good.* Is that
merely "made-up" by somebody? Or is that assertion—simply
speaking—true, independent of what anybody thinks? If love is
intrinsically good, then that goodness is not simply superimposed upon
the reality of love by anyone. Such a superimposition is obviously too
extrinsic and contradictory to the claim is that love is intrinsically good.

In contrast, if someone convinces others that hatred towards some other
religion or racial group is somehow "good," thereby imposing his own
meaning onto others, is that person really being authentic? In the first
sense, yes, but not in the second.

In the text below, I want to investigate the psychological consequences that follow if, outside of the Sartrean worldview, there also exists inherent meaning of things in reality.

It is granted that even the best of us will—at least at one time or another—manipulate and abuse our fellow human beings, especially if they are weak and defenseless. What if the miseries of this world, so often human-caused, are themselves measured by the standards of justice and goodness and truth, or, in other words, by the standards of rationality?

Maurice de Wulf has this to say about Scholastic (Medieval) psychology. He states, "According to the medieval classification of the sciences, psychology is merely a chapter of special physics, although the most important chapter, for man, is a microcosm; he is the central figure of the universe."[124] The focus here is on the idea of the "microcosm," which ought to be rationally in accord to the "macrocosm" of the cosmos, that is, with the objective realities of justice and truth. Josef Pieper further explains this idea when he states,

> The ultimate perfection attainable to us, in the minds of the philosophers of Greece was this: that the order of the whole of existing things should be inscribed in our souls. And this conception was afterwards absorbed into the Christian tradition ion the conception of the beatific vision: 'What do they not see, who see Him who sees all things?'[125]

Pieper's idea does not necessarily have to be explained through the prism of God and religion, as it can just as well be expressed through a rational (and secular) psychology, side-by-side with philosophical realism. For one can ask: What it is that really fulfills persons? Is it really a life full of pleasures, going from one pleasure to the next? Or is there another measure altogether: goodness, beauty and truth?

Perhaps the first time you think about the idea of living from pleasure to pleasure, you may be taken aback.[126] What possible problem can there be with a carefree, pleasurable existence?* And yet, is this pleasurable world really worth the price, say, of giving up even self-sacrificing love and of truth? Of course, there is nothing wrong with pleasure simply in itself, but what if some pleasures can only be "purchased" at the price of love and truth? Is that kind of pleasure worth it? For example, what if our world is pleasurable but not real, like living in a drug-induced illusory pleasure palace? The next chapter will come back to this question of truth and examine its psychological significance.

*THE RATIONALITY OF PLEASURES AND AFFECTIVE RATIONALITY

Someone might object to my implying that following one's pleasure is somehow not fully rational. Isn't it, after all, reasonable to search for things in reality that can give one pleasure?

Of course, this approach is, as far as it goes, perfectly reasonable and rational. However, it is far less reasonable for someone to prefer one's own pleasures at the expense of what is authentically good and true, especially if a life of continuous pleasures never leads to personal fulfillment and genuine happiness. If so, one can then notice a hierarchy of rationality: it is surely rational to follow one's pleasures, but it is far more important (and reasonable) to submit to what is authentically good and true.

It is also important to stress that the affective realm—those psychic acts, such as joy and sorrow, that are "felt"—are not reducible to the pleasures of the subjectively satisfying. Just because something is "felt" does not necessarily mean it is subjective in the sense of being a "mere feeling." There are some feelings that are every bit as rational and reasonable as any intellectual operation, such as with the joy someone experiences upon witnessing a heroic act motivated out of love. The tendency toward depreciating the affective dimension of human nature is far stronger in philosophy than in psychology.

It has been the position of classical, rational psychology to distinguish two specifically personal kinds of powers: the intellect and the will, with the intellect primarily oriented to *what is the case*, and the will being oriented to *what is good*. In the next two chapters, both of these fundamental powers will be discussed, with Chapter 8 focusing on the relation between psychology and truth and Chapter 9 discussing the will, whose object is the good.

Chapter 8

Psychology, Truth and Personalism

The focus of this chapter concerns the power of the intellect to know truth and the significance of truth for psychology. I am not looking for evidence of truth that would satisfy the skeptic. I will instead presuppose this power, which, after all, is the pre-condition for the possibility of doing science in the first place. Science presupposes knowledge and truth. This presupposition, however, can be so implicit that one hardly reflects upon it and its implications for psychology. Oddly enough, one can believe in science while at the same time ignore or even explicitly deny that a person can know anything. It is worthwhile, therefore, to focus on knowledge and truth, noting their implications for human nature and for psychology.

This focus on truth—the knowing of things simply as they are in themselves— is related to but goes in a different direction from a mere interest in practicality and usefulness, as the latter is only interested in "what works." As already noted, there are philosophers who will try to collapse the distinction between truth and practicality by either ignoring truth altogether or by reducing it to expediency, such as with the philosophy of pragmatism of William James. However, it seems clear that one does not necessarily have to choose one or the other, as both approaches can be combined without any reduction of one to the other.

Still, one might suspect that an interest in truth betrays a certain Pollyanna approach—as with someone who naively assumes that people are motivated only by the highest ideals—as opposed to a legitimate interest with results in this practical age. Furthermore, psychology certainly has an appropriate interest in practicality with respect to its role in the counseling profession, where the primary theme is health and not truth. The argument of this chapter, however, is that counseling and therapy lose a tremendous ally—both theoretically and even practically—by completely eschewing (non-pragmatic) truth in favor of an exclusive interest in usefulness.

Truth has far greater importance for psychology than one might at first think. I am not just thinking of truth from the point of view of honesty in reporting empirical facts or with straightforwardly and candidly dealing with others, crucial for every discipline. There is something else: an interest and respect for truth as possessing a high value in itself. In ethics, this respect for truth is called truthfulness or veracity. An interest in truth and truthfulness* are crucial notions for the counseling profession. The claim here is that by taking an interest in truth *for its own sake*—that is, by *not* reducing truth to a mere pragmatic idea—a counselor will have a powerful practical weapon for his counseling work. It is one interest among others, of course. But it never should be forgotten or relegated to mere usefulness. Evidence for this point can be found in counseling, as one of the best practical outcomes for clients is for them to come into a right relation to reality. Not only is truth the gold standard for clients but for all of us as well. Without a right relation to truth, everyone will inevitably become isolated from reality and from others. Liars are in a miserable state because they are alienating and alienated. All this can be admitted while recognizing the legitimate claims of practical usefulness.

*DISTINGUISHING TRUTH FROM TRUTHFULNESS (VERACITY)

Truth refers to a relation between a person and reality. Specifically, it refers to the adequacy (or "correspondence") between some state of affairs (or fact) "out there" in reality and a person's adequate judgment about it. For example, if I judge that 2+2=4, what I assert corresponds to what really is the case, and so that judgment is true.

Obviously, an inadvertent error, such as when someone makes a simple mistake, in addition, does not imply any attack on the veracity of the person. Truthfulness then differs from truth. While truth refers to the adequacy of judgments to reality, a person's proper response to the truth—respecting it and taking it seriously—is a moral value, which is truthfulness. Notice that respect for truth, which is truthfulness, is simultaneously tied to having respect for other persons. For if I lie to someone, I not only disrespect truth, I also disrespect that person.

This focus on truth and truthfulness provides a bridge for uniting the psychological sphere with what is distinctly personal. Truth is itself uniquely personal insofar as only persons can know and respond to what is true. Appreciating what is true completely transcends the animal realm and is utterly crucial for psychology. In what follows, I want to give six reasons for taking the psychological significance of truth seriously.

First, consider what psychologists (and philosophers) say about being in a right relation to reality and truth. The philosopher Robert Roberts says that the experiences of psychologically sane people "lack one of the crucial marks of psychological disease, namely that of distorting reality."[127] The psychiatrist Scott Peck states, "Psychotherapy is a light-shedding process par excellence."[128] And even Sigmund Freud—who theoretically denies not only freedom but also any transcendent rationality obtaining between the human beings and reality—says that "neurosis does not deny the existence of reality, it merely tries to ignore it; psychosis does ignore it and tries to substitute something else for it."[129]

Second, the importance of truth in psychotherapy can also be grasped by looking at its contrary opposite, lying. Freud's insight into lying led to one of his greatest discoveries: the phenomenon of repression. Adult repression essentially involves a certain kind of lying, which one philosopher, Dietrich von Hildebrand (1889-1977), calls "constitutive lying," or lying to one's self.[130] A simple example will help illustrate this connection. As many know, in Freud's early career, he investigated female hysterics, no doubt at some point asking them why they were so upset. Well, let us imagine one of them saying through her bitter tears *because 2+2 equals 4!* This response is clearly psychologically disordered, insofar as something like a simple mathematical formula is far too neutral and innocuous to motivate much of anything, especially some extreme affective response as hysteria. Something else was obviously at play. And yet, as Freud no doubt rightly surmised, this woman was clearly not intentionally lying to him. Rather, she was lying to herself, somehow repressing the true reason for her emotional state and displacing that emotional discharge onto something else, perhaps less threatening to her. Lying is closely connected to truth, presupposing truth.

Notice with the above example that persons cannot even begin to work on many psychological difficulties if they do not yet know what the real problem is. Knowing the problem obviously implies knowing the truth about it, which seems to be the necessary—even if not the sufficient—condition for the possibility of dealing with the problem. It was already noted in the last chapter how many psychological issues, such as anxiety, can be relatively impervious to rationality and insight. Insight is then not sufficient for overcoming such issues. But it is a crucial beginning.

Third, one wonders whether an interest in truth and the discovery of meaning—including ultimate meaning—ought to be considered as one of the explicit goals of psychological therapy. For example, could counselors really be satisfied with their clients living in a continuously happy drug-induced dream world, à la Aldous Huxley's *Brave New World*? Is such a world really worthy of them as persons? Is not this approach too steep a price for happiness and contentment? Or, perhaps better, whether this kind of "happiness," purchased at the price of truth, is in the end even happiness at all? I think it is not, and those settling for that state of affairs are really settling for what will slowly, or quickly, over time, lead to utter despair.

If living in a continuous illusory pleasure palace is not the end of therapy or of life, what is? Certainly, one end is to develop stratagems for successfully living life, which in turn could lead to some kind of psychological peace and equilibrium. Another goal is to be freed from the miseries of the "bad fruits" of psychological disorder, such as anxiety, obsessions, addictions, compulsions and so forth. But dealing with them also includes confronting the roots of these disorders in the "light" of what is true and real.

Such roots could certainly refer to family history and present relationships. It could also include an attitude towards meaning, including ultimate meaning, either in its origin or in its effect. There is obvious psychological fallout with respect to all of these factors, including ultimate meaning, especially if one thinks that the world and one's life are meaningless.

Someone could respond: *what is important to me is just getting through the day, dealing with concrete problems of relationships and addictions, as opposed to some abstract "truth."* The strength of this objection is correlated to the significance of being protected from the real miseries of the world. The more thematic these miseries are, the stronger this objection appears. And who doesn't need this protection, especially when sickness, failure, rejection, and death inevitably enter our life? During those times, having a reason for life and for suffering become crucially important. Thus, Victor Frankl paraphrases Nietzsche by noting, "Those who have a 'why' to live, can bear with almost any 'how'."[131] As a Nazi death camp survivor, his point was not cheaply bought, as he noticed how many people who despaired in the camp gave up and died. The "how" is important, but so is the "why."

Fourth, what is it about truth that makes it so important for persons? This importance is something more than mere pragmatism, that things work better if people are honest. Of course, that is true, but it also misses something that is far more fundamental and vital: the beauty and greatness of truth and how it can warm our little black hearts. Truth and truthfulness ought to be loved simply in themselves. Whether reality is ultimately beautiful or ugly, meaningful or despairing, good or evil, it is important and great to know its truth simply in itself. Animals are not built for truth, but persons are. It is our birthright.

Fifth, if the object of psychology is the *psyche*, two distinct senses of that term could be distinguished, referring either to the whole or to only one dimension of our psychological life. The first sense (of *psyche*) includes only the lower dimension of this life, that is, the needs, instincts, passions, emotional insecurities, immaturities, and neurotic responses a person might have. The second sense refers to a person's whole psychological life, that is, *psyche* and the rational/personal dimension of a person's life, which we can call *logos*. *Logos* involves an orientation to what is true and authentically good.

The second meaning sees *psyche* in the context of *psyche/logos* as two dimensions of one unified psychological reality. This second sense is, in my view, a more complete and accurate understanding of human nature and, consequently, of psychology. Psychologists, of course, have to do justice to our instincts, needs, compulsions, and defenses. But there is something else: rationality or *logos*, which is an orientation that persons have toward truth. That, too, is part of our nature and should be taken into account in our understanding of the human person, even if it is also true that we as human beings do not always apply or live up to it.

This orientation towards truth and rationality is what is uniquely constitutive of persons, and the discipline of psychology needs to take it into account. The result will be a psychological life in a broader, more accurate and robust sense. What this *logos* dimension implies is monumental: that human beings are actually persons instead of merely the highest of the higher-order animals, insofar as only persons are open to truth and respond adequately to transcendent reality.

Sometimes psychologists will identify human psychological life with only the first sense of *psyche* (the lower dimension of human nature), and then attempt to explain the "rational" dimension of human nature by immanent, psychological structures excluding all transcendent relations built on truth. However, the reality of the second sense of *psyche* (including *logos*) means that any reflexive temptation of psychology to explain *all* human motivation in terms of self-enclosed psychological categories—such as superego for conscience, Wise Old Man for God, instinctual sublimation for love, cultural norms for ethics, and biochemistry for rational intentionality—needs to be critically evaluated. Why? Because it substitutes immanent psychological and biological/biochemical (empirical) categories for personal, transcendent realities.[132] There is also something else at stake: conscience, authentic love, genuine ethics, God and rational intentionality. This second group of categories cannot be explained immanently, outside of a relation with what is transcendent, that is, going beyond the realm of the self to correspond to *what is* and *what ought to be.*

Let me grant that the first set of categories—Wise Old Man, instinctual sublimation, cultural norms, etc.—are real psychological phenomena, which can operate independently of their respective transcendent correlates. They are objects of legitimate psychological interest, especially since they are not explained in terms of any transcendent referent. Thus, what is left are immanent, psychological and sociological explanations.

It is also granted that each set of phenomena (for example, Wise Old Man for the transcendent, living God) can easily be confused with one another in some particular instance. Still, they are not reducible to each other nor even remotely close to each other in their own (metaphysical) kind of being. So the lower reality surely ought not to be used reflexively to explain the higher, unless, of course, psychologists want to make specifically philosophical arguments to justify this reductionism.

It is far more accurate to human nature to remember both dimensions of our psychological life, including *logos*. To systematically forget, ignore, explain away and reduce the *logos* (or the rational) dimension of human nature to (the first dimension of) the *psyche* is in effect to ignore our personal nature, thereby doing violence to that nature. We are first and foremost persons—oriented to truth and to what is authentically good—which also helps us to identify our vocation as persons: to be in a right relation to truth and goodness.

Finally, sixth, psychologists—as well as everyone else—will at least implicitly measure psychic acts and responses against the background of the adequacy of their responses to the truth about reality. This kind of judgment is at the heart of rational psychology, introduced above in Chapter 7. I now want to develop this idea—the adequacy of our responses to reality—since practically everyone at one time or another will use this kind of psychological reasoning. Even though it is an approach that has been superseded by the methodology of empirical psychology, it is hardly extinguished in modern psychology. In fact, it is implicitly used even by those psychologists who otherwise think that the empirical method is exclusively appropriate for the discipline of psychology. In contrast to a straightforward empirical *description* of facts, our volitional (going back to our will) and affective (going back to what is essentially "felt") responses can also be *prescriptively* measured by what ought to be, according to some rational measure.

Rational psychology can be exemplified by looking at several instances of how it is organically and implicitly applied practically by everyone. Consider the following contrast: on the one hand, imagine a gun battle raging outside. In that circumstance, a person's affective response of fear for going out into the line of fire is perfectly rational, and no one thinks (rightly) that there is any kind of strange psychological overlay. However, now suppose that instead of a battle or any other kind of objective threat, the day is sunny and peaceful with no hint of danger. Yet despite this, a person has an extreme and persistent fear of going outside. This fear is, of course, evidence of the psychological disorder of agoraphobia. Why? Because our emotional reaction *should* somehow reflect the actual degree of danger, and when there is no danger, there should be no fear. The rational measure at stake in this case obviously has everything to do with the disordered emotion and nothing to do with morality. This is obviously a purely psychological issue.

Consider now other psychological structures, such as virtue signaling, moral substitutes, value blindness, scapegoating, and blunting of conscience. In contrast to the above agoraphobia example, these structures have an obvious negative moral quality to them, and yet they are also all rich sources of psychological investigation. Why? Because the kind of being these structures possess is only psychological, that is, in the sense of being merely a product of someone's thinking. There is no correlation to reality. And these psychological structures are all "exposed" as being disordered and morally compromised when someone seriously compares what these structures envision as true with authentic moral goodness, that is, with what is really true about certain people, who really are morally good. In fact, it will be hard to discover the disordered psychological quality of these responses unless one first sees them in the light of authentic morality.

Finally, consider how the themes of truth and rational psychology can shed light on such vexing problems as anorexia nervosa, body dysmorphic disorder (BDD), body integrity identity disorder (BIID) and gender dysphoria. Dr. Michelle Cretella explains

> a girl with anorexia nervosa has the persistent *mistaken* belief that she is obese; a person with body dysmorphic disorder (BDD) harbors the *erroneous* conviction that she is ugly; a person with body integrity identity disorder (BIID) identifies as a disabled person and feels trapped in a fully functional body. Individuals with BIID are often so distressed by their fully capable bodies that they seek surgical amputation of healthy limbs or the surgical severing of their spinal cord. Dr. Anne Lawrence, who is transgender, has argued that BIID has many parallels with GD [gender dysphoria].[133]
> [Emphasis added].

Notice the rational psychological expressions—"mistaken" and "erroneous"—in the above passage. What is it that justifies these terms, if anything? As already noted (Chapter 7), Sartre collapses the distinction between first and second nature, making these kinds of evaluations radically intolerable. Whose meaning are we talking about? Authenticity in Sartrean philosophy means defining yourself in the way you chose, in radical freedom. In contrast to this view, I want to apply the distinction between first and second nature by broadening out the notion of "first nature" to refer not only to ontological "givens" (such as basic personal powers of intellect and will or animal powers of sense perception and instinct, as well as being biologically male or female) to also include simple truths about a person, such as that they are biologically healthy or sick, fat or thin. Would it not be a recognition of psychological health to be in a right relation to obvious, simple facts about oneself, whatever they are?

Psychologists will often face the difficult problem of wanting to be affirming and non-judgmental towards people and their conditions, as well as to try to help them. But what does *helping* mean? It perhaps could mean to do anything they can to try to change reality to fit their psychological state, which is a psychological correlate to the philosophical notion of idealism. It could, however, also mean the opposite of trying to help these people face what really is the case, the truth about who they are, which is a psychological correlate to realism. For example, someone who possesses a "fully functional body" (first nature) perhaps *ought* not to identify one's self as being disabled. Rightly understood, this *ought* is clearly not moral in nature; it is a rational, though non-moral, *ought*. In that example, a person's conscious evaluation is not in keeping with the truth of the matter, which is that this person is actually physically healthy. Therapy could then consist of helping the person come to see the truth of the matter and the psychological reasons for the misinterpretation.

Furthermore, all this can be presented without the slightest hint of condemnation. For, after all, it was already admitted that this is a psychological and not a moral problem, which needs to be psychologically addressed.[134] To address the problems that Dr. Cretella brings up as if they were first and foremost moral would be unjust and psychologically destructive. But that does not mean that such problems are still not psychologically disordered. Thus, this set of problems are in a very different category from the above responses of virtue signaling and moral blindness, which first and foremost possess a definite (negative) moral quality, as well as being psychologically disordered.

This idea of the adequacy of our psychic acts and responses to reality is the centerpiece of rational psychology. As already noted, it is a view that was theoretically superseded with the advent of empirical psychology in the late nineteenth century. Superseded, however, does not mean completely bypassed, as our earlier quotes from Freud and others suggest. I think a theoretical home for rational psychology should be *explicitly* affirmed by contemporary psychology, even if it is foreign to a rigorous empirical methodology, insofar as rational psychology involves measuring responses— not only according to some empirical standard (weight, color, width, etc.)—but also according to other rational measures (truth, value, goodness, etc.).

Someone could object: *the discipline of psychology is not merely interested in persons being truthful, it is also interested in the truth of empirical data. In that sense, contemporary psychology is already interested in the rational measure of empirical truth.* So, as this objection goes, psychology is already doing what it is I am advocating: having rational measures for psychological phenomena.

This objection has a point, and to answer it, two dimensions of truth can be distinguished: the first refers to what can be called "horizontal" truth: being true in the sense of describing the facts accurately "over against us," out there, so to speak, in reality. For example, one could say *grief has x number of typical stages* (whatever x is), or *someone with post-traumatic stress disorder is characterized by x symptoms* (whatever those symptoms are), and so forth. This horizontal sense is exclusively about rationally describing reality. Thus, the point of this horizontal sense of truth is to be purely descriptive, to what "is" the case.

There is, however, a "vertical" dimension of psychological truth that is prescriptive, that is, referring to what ought to be according to some rational plan, as opposed to merely what "is" the case. For example, *agoraphobia is characterized by **excessive** fear of going outside* or *a moral substitute*[135] *is characterized by someone projecting a moral significance onto something that is **really** (in truth) objectively neutral in importance.* The terms "excessive" in the first statement and "really" in the second indicate comparative measures (similar to the earlier terms in the above quote by Dr. Michelle Cretella, "mistaken" and "erroneous"). Even the assertion that one ought to be truthful to the actual scientific facts is actually *prescriptive* (going back to this second vertical meaning) as well as descriptive (horizontal meaning), which only describes what is the case.

Thus, besides this horizontal sense, there is also a vertical meaning of truth, referring again to a person being adequate in his response according to some rational measure of what ought to be—given the nature of the thing at stake—as opposed to what is the case. This rational order can refer to some order of morality, to the objective hierarchy of value in general (including its non-moral senses), or it can refer to various other kinds of non-moral, non-value measures. Some are summarized below:

1. Difficulties with the objective "theme" (that is, the main point or governing idea) of a situation, such as a professor going on a political rant when he or she ought to be teaching philosophy or literature.

2. Confusing basic facts, such as when someone who is starving thinks of herself as obese, or when someone is scared of going outdoors on a perfectly peaceful, sunny day.

3. Mis-understanding the basic nature of things, including the nature of one's own body, such as when someone thinks they are female when in fact they are biologically male.

4. Confusing parts for wholes, such as when a person looks at what is good exclusively through the lens of pleasure, politics, status, economics or power, and then absolutizes them when they are not absolute.

It is, however, not just any misinterpretation of reality that is of interest to rational psychology. Rational psychology is especially interested in those misinterpretations whereby a person receives some surreptitious, psychological benefit from the confusion. Uncovering a person's real motivation is a first step to psychological health.

This prescriptive "ought"—in all its differing manifestations—is especially found in the vertical dimension of truth, not merely in its horizontal sense. Thus psychology ought not to be exclusively attached only to this first, horizontal and purely descriptive meaning of facts. It also needs to recognize a second, vertical or prescriptive sense whereby one measures a psychological response according to various kinds of rational measures.

It was noted above that this important rational dimension of psychology has been neglected but not completely forgotten, as it is at least implicitly found in contemporary psychology. I might here mention where this dimension is explicitly and thematically found: with Dante (*The Divine Comedy*) and C. S. Lewis (*The Great Divorce*) in literature, Aristotle (*Nichomachean Ethics*), D. von Hildebrand (*Graven Images: The Substitutes for a True Morality*) and Max Scheler (*Ressentiment*) in philosophy, as well as St. Thomas Aquinas (*Summa Theologica*) in philosophy and theology. They have all investigated these themes in their respective disciplines with great *psychological* acuity. In my view, there is no good reason why contemporary psychology should cede this interesting line of psychological investigation to other disciplines. On the contrary, psychology has much to learn from them, just as its own empirical dimension has much to add to them to achieve a synthetic (or unified) vision of the primary object of psychological studies: the conscious life of the human person.

The overall theme of these later chapters concerns the focus on a person's higher nature, oriented to *logos*, without, of course, denying the lower nature of *psyche*. *Logos* is continuously presupposed—insofar as only persons can do science—but rarely reflected upon by contemporary psychology. Classical philosophy has identified two specifically personal powers of the soul: intellect and will. This chapter has focused on the intellect and a person's orientation to truth. The next chapter concerns freedom.

Chapter 9

The Reality and Psychological
Significance of Freedom

This chapter will further unfold the nature of freedom, give a sustained argument for its existence and consider its psychological significance. So far, a few aspects of the nature (or essence) of freedom have been discussed, such as that it is voluntary in nature, not determined by either external or internal factors, referring to a first or uncaused cause, and whose soul is an inner response that could then lead to an attempt to change some fact about the state of the world, and so forth. But I have not given any kind of argument for its real existence. For, after all, we could in principle know a lot of things about the nature of something, and yet still conclude that any being fitting that description does not exist. For example, atheists have to know something about the nature of an absolute being—as being all-powerful, all-knowing and the unconditioned ground for all being—as a necessary condition for the possibility of denying the existence of such a being. They could even grant strictly necessary, essential connections within the essence structure of the Divine Nature, such as that only an all-knowing being can be all-powerful. They just think that no real being actually exists corresponding to that idea. Something similar could be said about freedom: we can know all sorts of things about what freedom is; it just does not exist.

So far, only the reasoning of a common sense person was considered, who exclaims: *isn't it obvious that persons are free?* This is not enough for philosophers, who want to find evidence for positions, including conclusive evidence if possible. More importantly for this text, it is not enough for psychologists, insofar as many explicitly deny (Freud, Skinner) or at least ignore (introductory psychology textbooks) its existence.

Although the common sense person assumes freedom, actual evidence for its existence can be surprisingly difficult to explicitly and unambiguously identify, insofar as we all may have a tendency to be far more open to external manipulation than at first thought. We often do not notice when we are being externally manipulated from without, instead of freely willing from our own personal center. Things that go by the name of freedom could easily go back to something less. Perhaps the explanation for a person's action largely goes back to social pressure, following the crowd, one's upbringing, and being manipulated by clever advertisers and mass media than by anything coming from our freedom. Even if there is a dimension of freedom in some act, individual responses could still be reasonably interpreted in other ways.

Not only are the so-called acts of the will often better explained through various external influences, there are also internal influences upon the soul, such as with needs and instincts. It was noted in the last chapter that psychologists will often think of *psyche* as implying that all human motivation is captured by looking exclusively at instinctual urges and needs, and consequent sublimation from them. And, furthermore, when it comes to actually explaining motivation, it often pays to attend more to what people actually do than what they say. How many people are *really* motivated by a higher motivation of truth and goodness, especially when it is in conflict with their own self-interest? We are all tempted to make compromises and fool ourselves by "dressing up" our own motivation. Theorists might be more correct, at least generally speaking, to just presuppose a lower motivation of needs and instincts to explain human motivation. Thus, intellectuals who then explain freedom as if it is reducible to some kind of determinism may be surprisingly accurate with predicting actual behavior.

It is also easy for theorists to reduce the will to other powers insofar as they can be confused and intermix with each other. C. S. Lewis gives one example of such a possible mixing when a witness sees someone drowning in angry water. That observer could possibly save the other, but (let us say) at a real risk to his own life. Then Lewis states, "You probably want to be safe much more than you want to help the man who is drowning, but the Moral Law tells you to help him all the same...The thing [that is, your intellect and conscience] that says to you, 'Your herd instinct [to naturally want to help others] is asleep. Wake it up,' cannot itself be the herd instinct."[136] Lewis uses this example to first identify the "herd instinct" and then distinguish it from the will. My point is that this relation between instinct and will in concrete instances may be so close as to be easily confused.

Consider also numerous other instances when we simply acquiesce to our instincts, similar to animal voluntariness. This acquiescence is not merely reducible to instincts, but it remains close, especially when it becomes more and more automatic. Perceptive people know the more they follow their lower instincts, the stronger these instincts become and the weaker their experience of their own will. When this happens, the will tends to sink, at least experientially, into instinct.

I want to first unfold further what personal freedom is, so as to identify exactly what I am looking for from our common lived experience. Once identified, I then want to find examples where this experience of freedom is as unambiguously given as possible, ruling out as far as I can other possible interpretations of the phenomena. Towards that end, I will give examples of free action from people who are especially awakened to themselves, not of those who are spiritually asleep (where confusion is far more likely). Finally, the psychological significance of this power of willing will be investigated.

Freedom of will refers to the power of a person to be a first or uncaused cause. As was noted earlier (Chapter 5), free will is voluntary insofar as this power originates *internally* from within the person, as opposed to being just a link in some *external* causal chain in which energy is merely transferred from without, such as a rock on a hill causing other rocks further down to slide. Voluntary action, however, can apply either to persons or to animals, as with both cases, the principle of some action lies within the being itself. With personal freedom, however, the principle of its action not only lies within that being, it is also not determined from within, that is, from instincts. This is what distinguishes personal and animal voluntariness, insofar as the voluntariness of animal behavior is determined from within. Animals cannot go against their own instincts. If there exists a conflict of instincts, animals will simply go with the strongest. Persons, in contrast, are neither determined from without—as mere matter is determined from without—nor from within, insofar as they can go against their own instincts.

When I say that freedom is not determined, this is not to suggest that it is thereby not motivated. Of course, a free act has to be motivated insofar as it is always "about something" (that is, intentional), and it is this intentional object which gives us the intelligible reason for the willing. Thus, someone goes to the store to buy batteries because they are "good" for being able to power our flashlights. Reasons give freedom rationality in being ordered to what is and to what is good.

This being ordered by some motivating object insofar as it is good does not mean a person must then always will what is the "good" in some objectively real sense. The good here only means that which is positively important, which can go either in the direction of what is genuinely fulfilling and authentically good or towards what is merely subjectively satisfying. Thus, any individual free act will be on a continuum from what is rational to what is evil and irrational. Even a wicked person is motivated by the "good" of his own pride and lust for power.

Nor does a person necessarily have to will the "good" in some deterministic (whether external or internal) sense. Since freedom is rational and rationality requires motivation, the nature of this motivation is that of an invitation. It cannot be a determining cause, as this would destroy freedom. More importantly, the idea that a motive is a determining cause goes against our lived experience. For example, just because a person is motivated to, say, buy an expensive watch does not mean he will necessarily do it. The condition for the possibility of willing anything is that a person be motivated. He could think: *I really want this watch. But, no. I've got other more pressing expenses coming up. I can't afford it.* Everyone has these kinds of experiences all the time. Not only does motivation not take away freedom (as if determining it), it is a necessary condition for its possibility.

There are two dimensions of personal freedom.[137] The first refers to the power to will to change a fact about the state of the world, such as, for instance, attempting to change a fact about a person drowning to her not drowning. While this kind of freedom is in itself unlimited, in the sense that our willing can, in principle, refer to any known state of affairs (or fact), our actual physical or mental powers are not. Thus, a person may completely will with all his might to save another from drowning, but he may still lack the strength to successfully save that other.

The second dimension refers to the power simply to inwardly say "yes" or "no" to a state of affairs. This second dimension is at the heart of the first dimension, dealing with some action, insofar as this inward willing is the "inner soul" of free action. Thus, the first dimension presupposes the second, but the second can exist without the first. For example, a person hears the tragic news that another has inoperable cancer and is unconscious, having only hours to live. There is nothing more this person, or anyone else can "do" for that other to, say, cure or even care for him, going back to an application of the first dimension of freedom. But the second dimension is, in this instance, still operable, as one can always give an inner response of loving concern.

Notice that the person receiving the news of something like inoperable cancer—in effect, a kind of death sentence—can respond in basically two ways: either accept it as the will of God, even in the face of his own anger and misery. Or he can unite his will with his feelings of anger concerning this cruel news and revolt against God. Notice that in the first instance, this "felt" (affective) response of anger is something different and even contrary to his willed (volitional) response,* going in a diametrically opposite direction from that person's will. This obviously implies that a person's volitional response is something distinct from his affective response. In fact, a volitional response is actually not "felt" at all. This is why a volitional response can oppose one's own feelings. Furthermore, our affective responses arise spontaneously within us, and thus in that sense they are outside of our freedom. In contrast, our volitional response always begins from our free, spiritual center. This is why the volitional response is a "first" or uncaused cause.

*HOW VOLITIONAL RESPONSES CAN DEVELOP CHARACTER AND CHARACTER CAN AFFECT INDIVIDUAL AFFECTIVE RESPONSES

Volitional and affective acts are two distinct yet related kinds of responses. Whereas affective responses are not within our direct volitional power, I can directly will a volitional response, such as, for example, jumping into a pool to try to save a child in distress. Still, there is a sense in which affective responses can be freely engendered, not directly via the will, but *indirectly*, insofar as our free choices build our psychological and moral character, which in turn largely determine what is affectively experienced.

Thus, it is hardly news that the kind of person we eventually become is greatly determined by our free decisions in life. Each of us becomes, via our freedom, either trustworthy and loving or untrustworthy and vicious. Although I cannot directly will to have a good character, I can directly will those individual acts and responses that in turn build a certain kind of character. And in turn, the character which develops in me then helps determine what kind of affective responses I spontaneously engender. It is not surprising that someone with a morally good character will not only see what is objectively good, but will it, and then (affectively) come to love it. But someone who is vicious will not only not love the good, he may not even see it, or if he does, hate it.

This is especially the case with respect to a person's moral life. It is one thing to know what is authentically good, but not necessarily will it. It is another thing to will it, but not necessarily love it. And it is yet another thing to know, will and love it all together. This is the end game of a person's moral transformation. It is also what leads to a person being psychologically integrated and whole. This is self-determination, referring (Chapter 7) exclusively to our second nature and not at all to our first nature.

These two dimensions of the will (again, willing to change a fact about reality as well as an inner "yes" or "no" response) are clearly given in our lived experience, so it makes no sense to outright deny them. If someone is interested in undermining freedom, instead of merely denying the experience, it is better to follow Sam Harris' suggestion[138] and call it illusory. He—together with famous psychologists like Sigmund Freud and B. F. Skinner before him— argues that what are typically thought of as free acts when investigated are explained by other realities beyond our will. Thus, he thinks freedom is explained by the circumstances of one's life, and these circumstances ultimately are due to "luck," such as with the parents we have, the religion we are born into, the cultural circumstances that surround our life, our biochemistry, and so forth.

It would, of course, be foolish to think of these influences as nothing. Harris makes use of an earlier distinction already discussed: the role of causes and conditions (Chapter 5) that help form our life. It is obvious that all these factors really do help form our psychological life and being, which can also be empirically necessary conditions for the possibility of any kind of willing at all. One wonders, however, if these causes and conditions can simply replace our freedom.[139]

Perhaps the real question is not whether our *being* is uncaused (our being is obviously the effect of many causes and conditions), but whether our *choices* are free and uncaused. Our *being*—including our personality—is obviously given to us by our parents, ancestors and the circumstances of our life. No doubt we have all had the experience at one time or another of congratulating ourselves for things that really are the result of our cultural and familial upbringing and conditioning. For example, I haven't taken anything that did not belong to me since I was a child. Is this because I am a superior human being, or is it mostly just a product of my family, financial and cultural circumstances? Put another way, how many convicted thieves presently in jail today would be there if they had my upbringing? Conversely, would I have been able to avoid jail if I had had their upbringing?

So, there really is something to grant with Sam Harris' argument against freedom: the role of causal factors, together with cultural and religious conditions, are tremendously important in forming all of our lives, giving crucial context to our free choices. He is also right that what we think are free acts can be confused with these causes and conditions in particular cases. But the question is this: do these factors explain much, or do they form all of our psychic life and choices? Am I really only the product of my circumstances, or is there *something else*? Perhaps I really do give myself too much credit for not being a thief. On the other hand, it also seems true that I need to freely cooperate with my cultural upbringing.

My aim is to make evident the real existence of this *something else*, which is freedom. It seems to me that its reality is not only given; my freedom is even inwardly self-evidently given, despite the fact that it is often obscured by other factors and influences. As I want to show, freedom is not only self-evidently given; it is given with certainty. To show this, I need to find an experience that clearly goes back to freedom and which is as distinct from the circumstances (conditions and other causes) of our life as possible. Furthermore, since this book is primarily meant as a psychology text using philosophical argumentation,

I need to find an approach that is more experiential and less strictly metaphysical and abstract, going back to our psychological lived experience.

Empirical science cannot help me here, insofar as inner psychic acts are not empirically given, including free acts. Rather, it is to our inner lived experience that I can find an unambiguous experience of freedom. I want to identify this "givenness of freedom"—especially by distinguishing it from things which can be confused with it, such as other causes, conditions and instincts—by making five points.

It seems to me that the real problem with seeing free acts is not with their self-evidence, but rather with properly identifying them from among the welter of other psychic phenomena. Then after making these distinctions, I will present my argument, which—after various clarifications and identifications—is in actuality reducible to an appeal to a direct seeing of the psychic reality of freedom.

First, recall what was already said (Chapter 4) about self-presence, and how it refers to the subjective dimension of a bipolar[140] psychological experience, with the other (objective) dimension being intentional or object-oriented conscious experience. This subjective dimension is always present when we are intentionally oriented to conscious objects, and it can be either strengthened or decreased. Someone could have the subjective life of someone like a John Paul II or a Prince Valium, that is, intensely self-present or hardly present to ourselves at all.

Second, in order to establish the experience of freedom, it would be helpful to intensify our self-presence so we can be more aware of what comes *from us*, as opposed to what merely comes *to us* from outside sources. For, after all, confusion more easily happens when people are distracted and drawn off from themselves, as opposed to those who especially actualize themselves by standing in their own center.

Third, how can this increase of self-presence be achieved? There are two basic ways. One is for a person to take any intentional experience, whether of thinking or promising or loving or hating, and go to the subjective pole of that experience to find one's self and further actualize it. For example, there really is a difference between making a casual, thoughtless promise as opposed to a serious promise, where I say, "No! *I* promise this." Although all intentional acts reveal at the subjective pole the conscious subject performing them, some intentional acts disclose the person more readily and perfectly than others. For example, I can increase my subjective self-presence by actively collecting myself to stand in my own center. I can voluntarily "gather myself up" to stand in my own center as I give myself over to some object. In other words, I can say to myself, "you're asleep and dissipated. Come to yourself! Wake up!"

Naturally, if the experience of "voluntarily coming to myself…to stand in my center" is possible at all, then freedom already exists. Since this ability is precisely what is being disputed and what I am here trying to establish, I will here discuss the second way.

The other way of "coming to one's self" concerns experiences that take me organically (or naturally) to myself and increase my self-presence. For example, think of some extraordinary experience of value, say, of beauty and goodness that deeply touches me. By coming in contact with that great and noble thing, a person naturally comes to himself. It is as if our personal center is especially awakened and actualized in this knowing relation with something great. Conversely, there are other experiences that are psychologically "deadening." Think of a person performing exactly the same action, say, on a production line for long periods of time. When some action is boring and monotonous, often the effect will be of a person becoming, at least to some extent, lost to himself.

Earlier (Chapter 2), one example of someone coming to himself from an experience of value was from the fairy tale *Beauty and the Beast*. The Beast falls in love with Belle and, in doing so, makes a rather surprising self-discovery: that he is actually not a beast at all, but a prince.

This fairy tale makes perfect psychological sense. It "rings true" because it exemplifies the psychologically significant experience of self-discovery. In coming into contact with something great—that is, with Belle—the Beast is led to actualize himself at a deeper level, acting more and more "prince-like," such that he becomes able to even sacrifice himself (in the Disney version) for her, which is exactly what real men do for their women.

So, there are two ways in which we can "come to ourselves": volitionally (*I am spiritually asleep. Wake up!*) and naturally or organically through some experience of goodness and value. The effect of both cases will be an intensified self-presence, which will allow us to better distinguish what goes back to me from what merely goes back to external causes and conditions.

Consider now another example: Sir Thomas More in Robert Bolt's play *A Man for All Seasons*. If you know the play, you might remember More's friend, the Duke of Norfolk, trying to persuade More to go along with the British nobility in acquiescing to Henry the Eighth's claim to be the supreme head of the Church of England. More saw this as a revolt against the proper authority of the Christian Church and declined, thus making a principled but extremely dangerous stand against the king (which will, in the end, cost More his life). Consider his reply to Norfolk, "I will not give in [to the king] because I oppose it—I do—not my pride, not my spleen, nor any of my appetites, but *I* do–-*I* [emphasis in text]!"[141] Here More is exactly aware of the possibility of confusing his instincts ("my spleen") from his will ("I—*I*"). But notice, we are not dealing with someone who is relatively asleep, like Prince Valium or the poor person on some monotonous assembly line. No, this is an example of someone awakened to himself, especially in the light of this threat to his own life as well as to what he thought were serious religious issues at stake.

Fourth, reflect on another way of getting at the difference between a volitional (free will) response from other psychic experiences which can be confused with it. For example, think of a mere instinctual reaction, such as the way a little girl plays with dolls. She "loves up" her doll all right…until sleepiness takes over, and then the doll will, half the time, end up on the floor while the girl sleeps on her bed. But a mature, loving mother will, on the contrary, volitionally face down her utter exhaustion, expending herself for the sake of her baby. Here one really sees the obvious difference between mere maternal instincts and the iron will of the mother. How could someone like Sam Harris miss this distinction?

Finally, (fifth), one wonders how such acts as evaluating evidence or promising or commanding—among many other psychic acts—could work without the will to evaluate, the will to promise or the will to command? As already noted, there is the possibility of performing these acts in a kind of un-reflected, "sleepy" state. *Wake up, man! Come to yourself!* The volitional act of "coming to yourself" is at times crucially important for the possibility of adequately performing all these other psychic acts. The volitional response does not just stand or fall on its own with no consequences for other psychic acts. No, many if not all the other psychic acts are similarly affected. In fact, our whole inner personal life—what was termed as *logos* above—is undermined if someone denies psychic freedom.

After this preliminary work of identifying, as exactly as possible, where the free acts are to be found, especially as distinguished from other causes, conditions and instincts which can be confused with them, now I can present my argument. It is not really an argument (or proof, that is indirectly establishing a conclusion through a premise or premises). It is rather a simple pointing to what is itself already directly given in our lived experience: that *I can freely say "yes" or "no" to a state of affairs.*

Earlier (Chapter 1, footnote 9), I mentioned how it is that "typically" causal connections are not directly intuited. This point characterizes all *empirical* causal connections. For example, fire causes smoke. I see that relation. I see it repeated, which leads me to believe that there is a causal relation between fire and smoke. However, I must admit (along with David Hume) that this connection is not directly intuited. Thus in "knowing" this causal relation I only have an inductive, inferential knowledge of it in that case, which could be reducible to mere associations and psychological expectation. Thus, for Hume, there is doubt whether causality even exists. Certainly, this kind of knowledge does not admit to anything like an absolute certainty.

Perhaps this lack of certain knowledge of the connection between fire and smoke is not enough to get me (or you) to doubt a real causal connection between them. But I still must admit with David Hume that the causal connection between fire and smoke is not intuited. Doubting this connection is possible, as well as all other empirical, causal connections.

This argument of Hume has undermined the belief that modern science had in causality, and it explains why B. F. Skinner wants to get away from thinking in terms of causes and effects, including the notion of freedom as being a first cause. But, does the analysis really destroy freedom?

I think not. For notice that inwardly saying *"yes" to a state of affairs* is not an empirical causal connection. Rather, all that I am doing is inwardly bringing into existence a "yes." If I can do this, I have the power of freedom. And to do this, all that is necessary is being present to myself (laterally) as the one performing this act. Again, in self-presence the really existing "I" is already given. Perhaps David Hume and B. F. Skinner can doubt all *empirical* causal connections because they are not, after all, directly intuited. But this inward connection of merely saying "yes" to a state of affairs is inwardly given and directly intuited. This is not an empirical connection.

Thus, I have certain knowledge of freely willing in a concrete act, such as when I inwardly and freely say a "yes" or "no" to some state of affairs. If I can freely will in even one case, it shows that I have the (ontological) power of being able to do this. That is all I want to establish: the power of freedom. While David Hume is right with respect to the absence of an intuited causal nexus being given in some (or any) *empirical* instance, he is wrong to assume that in *every* instance of causality, the causal nexus is missing.

Furthermore, I do not see how this volitional act is any more disputable than the existence of any of the other kinds of psychic acts, such as of promising or commanding, loving or knowing. If I can perform an act of promising or commanding, I can also inwardly say "yes" to what I promise or command and thereby affirm them. How is promising or commanding possible if I am not free to *will to promise* or *will to command*?

Even while granting the complexities of all the possible ambiguities, such as confusing willing with instincts or unconsciously following the crowd in some particular case, this obscurity is reduced and is eliminated when considering the case of persons who are collected, and who then inwardly will a "yes" or "no." Their "yes" or "no" to some state of affairs is not only possible, where all reasonable confusion is eliminated, it is even certainly given.

Now I want to turn to the psychological significance of freedom. Doing justice to this significance will yield still more insights into the real existence of freedom. My claim is that the reality of personal freedom is utterly foundational for properly understanding the nature of the human person and our psychological experience.

First, let us imagine someone accepting Harris' suggestion that everything, including all psychic acts and what is produced by them, is simply a matter of "luck," as he puts it.[142] What would be the psychological result of that acceptance? Is it not manifestly clear that the result would be sheer passivity, an ennui that could be psychologically unhealthy for everyone who seriously accepts and then actually applies that notion to their own life? For example, consider those personalities—stunted, fixated adults—who steadfastly refuse to act through themselves. Is this not a clear instance of immaturity? Most people would rightly hope that such persons will at some point "find themselves," and then grow up and mature and then begin to think and act in their own name. Consider this passage from Alan Wheelis, talking about psychoanalytic therapists,

> Toward the end of the analysis the therapist may find himself wishing that the patient were capable of more 'push,' more 'determination,' a greater willingness to 'make the best of it.' Often this wish eventuates in remarks to the patient: 'People must help themselves'; 'Nothing worthwhile is achieved without effort'; 'You have to try.'[143]

No one can fail to pick up the irony with such cases, especially if they come from psychoanalytic therapists who theoretically deny free will.[144]

Second, while it is impossible to will what one does not know, the converse relation is also true: we cannot know—at least with deeper realities and truths—without first wanting and actually willing to know. There exist many truths that are not so obvious and thus require effort and openness to evidence. This refers to scientific truths and especially to deeper truths of a religious, moral or metaphysical nature. For example, religious truth is often not simply an intellectual matter as it is also a matter of the will, insofar as one typically needs to be willing to search for what is true. Thus there is something "freedom-like" about knowledge, for a seeker of knowledge has to be "open to evidence" and willing to search actively for what is true.

Earlier in this text (Chapter 1), the obvious positive psychological effect of people thinking for themselves was discussed. Yet, without freedom, what sense does the notion of *thinking for oneself* make? For, after all, everyone would then be just the passive recipients of prior causes that would determine what we think. If we are just passive recipients, does that not also apply to Harris' own assertion that freedom is illusory? Would not his claim also be illusory because he has been merely caused to think it? Just because something is caused does not mean it is necessarily true, as sheer illusions can also be biochemically caused. Thus, causality alone is surely intelligible (as it can be known) but also non-rational. Something more and even other is needed for rationality, insofar as what makes a psychic act rational is its correspondence to reality. So, if Harris' view that freedom is determined is itself merely caused, and mere causation alone goes back to non-rational factors, does that not undermine the rationality of his own claim that freedom is determined?*

*DISTINGUISHING THE RATIONAL FROM THE NON-RATIONAL, THOUGH INTELLIGIBLE EXPLANATIONS FOR THINGS

Let us say I claim *there are dangerous snakes up in my attic!* Perhaps your initial response to this declaration is skepticism. For, after all, it is strange and rather surprising for snakes to be living in an attic. But then let us say I have no history of mental illness and that I add this: *both my friend and I have been lately up there looking for mice, and he vouches for me as to our actually having seen them. We noticed a hole in the attic where both mice and snakes could enter and exit the house. The snakes were apparently eating the mice.* Thus, I back up my original assertion with an actual sighting, verified by another who also saw them, together with presenting a reasonable theory of how and why snakes got into the house in the first place.

Now imagine a different story. *There are snakes in the attic!* But this time, I offer no rationale or independent verification for this claim. I rather assert that *while "tripping" on some hallucinogenic drugs, I had an "out of the body" experience of "seeing" enormous snakes with large red beady eyes and monstrous fangs in the attic!* Naturally, this second rendition hardly convinces anyone.

Why? Notice in both cases there are cause-and-effect sequences, as both sense perception and hallucinogenic experiences involve brain physiology and biochemistry. Both stories are, therefore, intelligible in the sense of possessing inner meaningfulness, which allows them to be at least understood. But only the first experience involves serious evidence, correspondence to reality and interpersonal confirmation, while the second does not. Hallucinogenic drug experiences are not a reliable source of transcendent knowledge of reality. Thus, it is the reasonableness of the first story that separates the two cases and not merely the cause-and-effect sequences alone, which characterizes both experiences.

Freud theoretically focuses only on the second kind of experience, excluding the first kind. He oddly assumes that all personal motivations ultimately go back to non-rational or even irrational factors, whose sources are determined by psychological and biological factors. However, even assuming the ubiquity of irrational human motivation (for the sake of the argument), Freud still has to presuppose intelligibility and rationality, which are the conditions for the possibility of investigating the nature of psychopathology, which is the rational study of the irrational. Psychopathology is not the irrational study of the irrational. And only beings possessing rational powers have the wherewithal to do science.

Harris' determinism (going back to luck) makes far more sense with respect to non-rational and irrational determining factors. But with respect to rational reasons for things, there is typically the need to look for evidence and then to volitionally accept that evidence when it is judged sufficient. Again, just as the will presupposes knowledge, the reverse is also true.

Finally, (third), morality becomes absurd without freedom. Where is the moral merit or the ethical responsibility for what is morally good without freedom? The condition for the possibility of performing any morally good or bad action is that the person performing the action be in some sense free. For example, everybody sees the moral greatness of an action of someone heroically risking his life in an angry, swollen river to save another out of love. But this heroic goodness is obviously missing with a log floating down a river that inadvertently saves a drowning person. What is the difference between these two cases? Freedom is found in the first case, but it is absent in the second. Without freedom, the moral significance of these two instances becomes indistinguishable, and the option of a morally good action becomes impossible.

The only escape for not granting the significance of freedom for psychology is by simultaneously not granting the significance of morality. This significance goes in two basic directions. On the one hand, how else can we explain the psychological experience of moral guilt? An earlier example was that of a person being haunted (from a bad conscience) after casually murdering another person. How can this—seriously and without reductionism—be explained outside of any moral sensibility? And how can any moral sensibility be explained outside of freedom?

On the other hand, there is the question of what genuinely fulfills a person. How can we do justice to what fulfills a person outside of any moral goodness?

Can a life of never-ending pleasure banquets and orgies, or even merely a life of a person continuously playing his or her favorite computer game, authentically fulfill a person? How do these things compare to the moral goodness of self-sacrificing love? To sufficiently answer such questions, a person must go to his or her depth, which in turn requires a *willingness* to go to his or her depth.

It seems that we cannot get rid of freedom without simultaneously getting rid of morality. Still, it may at first seem easy to get rid of morality, especially if it helps us smother (repress) our own bad conscience (well, at least on the surface of our psychic life). On the other hand, how will we respond when it is our turn to be the innocent victim of some moral injustice?

In fact, getting rid of freedom leads to undermining not just morality, but the basic rationality of any position. For, without freedom, why bother looking for rational evidence for positions? What does "looking" mean but the will to find what is rationally appropriate and due in some situations. This includes the truth about reality, which is the basis and motivation for all science as well as one's own intellectual position. It is far better for psychology to explicitly affirm our freedom instead of denying or ignoring its existence.

Chapter 10

Conclusion

The five major themes of this book are as follow:

First, one activity of philosophers is to investigate the beginnings and ends of things as well as first principles, including both what people think they are and what they really are. Every science, without exception, has first principles and beginning insights—or at least assumptions—which get their science going. One such principle for modern psychology is the idea that psychology is an empirical science. That psychology is an empirical science is so taken for granted today that it is considered a mere truism, worthwhile stating but not worthy of investigation. The real question, however, is whether it is *only* an empirical science. Yet, this exclusivity is what leading psychologists (B. F. Skinner, Sigmund Freud) explicitly assert, and psychological textbooks implicitly make, when they offer no other methodology besides the empirical method. These explicit assertions and implicit assumptions are two versions of psychological empiricism.

Chapters 2 & 3 investigated the adequacy of this empiricism claim. Granting the obvious importance of the empirical dimension of psychology, arguments were made that it does not justify the further claim that *all* of psychology is empirical. This is especially the case when the sciences do not really study, via any kind of direct intuition, the universal natures of things. What they rather do is observe concrete empirical realities and then apply the principle of induction, inferring indirectly to a general understanding of empirical realities. Mere inductive generalizations cannot in principle ever justify any strictly necessary assertion, including the claim that all psychology is empirical, as observations from concrete particulars alone do not yield insights into the universal nature of things.

Second, if the starting point of psychology is not to claim that it is a pure empirical science, just what is its actual starting point? What are its first principles and its starting points? Reflection on this topic reveals a familiar philosophical experience: everyone knows what the object of psychology is...until you ask them. This was the topic of Chapters 4 & 5, where various kinds of objects were investigated. The central theme uniting all these different kinds of objects is that psychology studies the idea of consciousness or at least to an orientation to conscious life, as well as to the causes and conditions for conscious life.

I also argued that it is not just psychic acts and the conscious self that are non-empirical, but also the products of these acts are all non-empirical as well. These products of psychic acts go in three general directions: in the direction of promises, commands, judgments and vows, all of which have a kind of derivative psychological reality, insofar as they are constituted by psychic acts. Then there are other products that are either partially psychologically produced (appearances) or completely psychologically produced (illusions). And finally, there are the meaningful, organic "fruits" of certain psychic acts, leading to joy or sadness, happiness or misery.

Third, this led to an investigation (Chapter 6) as to the place of empirical psychology in psychology. The nature and object of the empirical method, in general, was identified as the observation of sensible phenomena and an inductive generalization from them to establish universal laws or a general species knowledge. Concerning psychology, this method is especially helpful with respect to understanding those areas that go back to behavior: such as the biological causes and conditions of behavior, learning, development, social psychology, principles of conditioning, testing, kinds of mental illness and therapeutic solutions, etc.

Fourth, it was claimed that all these non-empirical dimensions of psychology not only exist, they encompass such an extremely large realm that the sciences and disciplines studying them include also philosophy, literature and theology. Psychological phenomena not only refer to dimensions observed scientifically from without, they are also experienced inwardly from within a person's naïve, lived experience. All these disciplines and experiences not only offer different perspectives to psychological truth, they also provide a unique and even irreplaceable psychological content that is largely and sometimes completely outside of what can be known (strictly speaking) via any scientific, empirical methodology. Scientific psychology (alone) knows nothing of our conscious life, as such a life is only experienced "from within."

In contrast, literature can focus on psychological truth "from within" by unfolding the inner experience of its characters. It also can focus on showing psychologically significant, universal truths via its individual stories. In contrast, empirical research only looks at psychological phenomena "from without," as it tries to achieve a generic understanding of reality from the point of view of a universal species or law established from observation and induction.

Philosophy too is interested in discovering universal laws, but primarily from insight or intellectual intuition into essence structures. Philosophy can grasp highly intelligible (philosophical) universal truths via intellectual intuition, which is a tremendous aid for understanding the prescriptive dimension of rational psychology (Chapter 8).

And finally (fifth), philosophy investigates a different dimension of psychology, pre-dating empirical psychology, called rational psychology. This kind of psychology measures psychic acts and responses, not *descriptively* according to what (empirically) is the case, but *prescriptively* according to what ought to be, as measured by various kinds of rational measures. Rational psychology was largely forgotten, at least in some explicit methodological sense in modern psychology. But it has never completely been extinguished. It is often implicitly appealed to by contemporary psychology, even if not thematically developed by it. Thus, in Chapters 8 & 9, the rational powers of intellect and will that specifically and uniquely evaluate our psychic, rational acts and responses were investigated. These rational powers were distinguished from both animal powers and mere forces in nature.

Notice with respect to the whole analysis of this book; there was never an appeal to even one empirical, psychological study. Nor am I aware of contradicting any strictly empirical, psychological or scientific study. And yet, at the same time, the topics discussed in this text are obviously of psychological interest.

It is high time for contemporary psychology to give up the notion that it is an exclusively empirical science. Something else is applicable: a philosophy of psychology, a psychology of literature and even of theology. And of course, there is also the tremendously important dependency of psychology on simple lived experience, including those dimensions of our lived experience that are outside of empirical observation (such as inner conscious experience), without which psychology would be strictly impossible. Psychology could exist without empirical science, but empirical psychology cannot exist without at least implicitly presupposing inner conscious states and the conscious subject.

These other sources of psychological insight, however, should not be considered as some competing psychological approaches. They rather can and should work in conjunction with empirical psychology to get a more complete and adequate vision of psychological realities.

Of course, psychology needs to continue its empirical dimension, but it also needs to open itself up to its other dimensions as well. In my view, there needs to be not only empirically oriented psychology courses, but also other classes on the psychological dimensions of philosophy, literature, and theology. This would go a long way in balancing what is presently off-kilter in contemporary psychology.

Notes

1 Later, I will call this philosophical psychological approach rational psychology.

2 An efficient cause refers to that through which something comes into being or changes. A final cause refers to the purpose or end of something. The end of teeth is the chew, the end or purpose of dentistry is to fix teeth, and so forth.

3 One particular school of psychology that especially sees the importance of and makes good use of philosophy is found at Mercy University. Paul Vitz, William Nordling and Craig Steven Titus employ what they call the "Meta-Model" of the person. They state,

> [T]he Meta-Model posits that psychology, philosophy, and theology are all sources of truth about the person. They make integrative and complementary contributions to a realist understanding of the person. These disciplines act as "lenses" for viewing the person and together provide the possibility of a richer, clearer vision of the person than is possible when only one lens is utilized.
> Paul C. Vitz, William J. Nordling, and Craig Steven Titus, *A Catholic Christian Meta-Model of the Person* (Sterling VA: Divine Mercy University Press, 2020), 4.

Another psychological program that is similarly open to philosophy, including a phenomenological approach, is at Franciscan University of Steubenville.

While there are good trends in both psychology and philosophy (such as with the flowering of personalism in philosophy), it remains true of course that both disciplines need to be approached carefully, which also helps explain the purpose of this book. Relativism (*truth and goodness are only what we think it is*), skepticism (*human beings cannot know truth*) and nihilism (*there is no ultimate meaning or truth*) are widespread in both fields. In fact, both relativism and skepticism can be found in other phenomenological approaches. Not every phenomenology is realist.

4 Kant does not maintain a total idealism—with everything coming from the mind—insofar as he admits to the receptivity of the sensuous intuition. But he held that without some further contribution from the mind, this intuition alone is insufficient for knowledge.

5 For example, James states, "The 'true,' to put it very briefly, is only the expedient in the way of thinking, just as the 'right' is only the expedient in the way of our behaving. Expedient in almost any fashion: and expedient in the long run and on the whole, of course."
William James, *Pragmatism* (New York: Macmillan, 1960), 86.

In contrast to William James, this text will investigate psychological phenomena without collapsing the distinction between the "true" and the "right" into the "expedient." that is, without simply reducing realism to pragmatism.

6 B. F. Skinner admits to this point (generally speaking) when he stated at the end of his life, "most scientific accounts of human behavior remain a matter of interpretation."
B. F. Skinner, *Upon Further Reflection* (New York: Dover, 1986), 19.

7 Bishop Robert Barron was asked what in his view is the greatest danger American society is facing today? His reply, "I would say it's the ideology of self-invention. What I mean by that is, this goes back to Nietzsche in the 19th century and comes up to Sartre in the 20th

century, Michel Foucault, people like that. It was once a very high academic thing, but now I think it's in almost every teenager in America: the view that truth is a function of my will, value is a function of my will." Bishop Robert Barron, "Bishop Robert Barron sets sights on America's secular culture," *Aleteia*, accessed July 1, 2021, https://aleteia.org/2018/06/11/bishop-robert-barron-sets-sights-on-americas-secular-culture/

[8] As evidence for this assertion, try looking up *freedom* or *free will* in the Index of your introductory psychology textbook. Odds are you won't even find a reference to them. If you do find such a reference, the content referenced will be minimal and tangential. There will be no serious, thematic investigation of them.

[9] To empirically grasp causal relations, one needs to see them "in the intellectual light" of the principle of causality, which is that *every change has a cause*. A pure empiric*ism*, strictly speaking, will not grant the principle of causality, thus undermining the notion of causality altogether. But, in a wider sense, psychology textbooks will use the language of causality all the time (despite their attempt at adopting a pure empirical approach). This approach (of using causality in a looser sense) is justified by B. F. Skinner, who states,

> The terms "cause" and "effect" are no longer widely used in science. They have been associated with so many theories of the structure and operation of the universe that they mean more than scientists want to say. The terms which replace them, however, refer to the same factual core [without the rationalist "baggage" of the principle of causality]. A "cause" becomes a "change in an independent variable" and an "effect" a "change in a dependent variable." The old "cause-and-effect connection" becomes a "functional relation" ... There is no particular danger in using "cause" and "effect" in an informal discussion if we are always ready to substitute their more exact counterparts.

B. F. Skinner, *Science and Human Behavior* (New York: Macmillan, 1953), 23.

Since I do not hold to either an implicit or explicit empiricistic position (empiric*ism*) and accept the principle of causality as a real principle, verifiable in exactly the same kind of way that mathematical and basic metaphysical principles (such as non-contradiction, identity, etc.) are justified, language acrobatics will not be unnecessary. Changes really do require causes to explain them, insofar as the world is intelligible and knowable. This is presupposed for all of science.

That, however, does not mean that we are always able to see the connection (nexus) between particular causes and effects directly. This is especially the case with empirical causal connections, which can only be empirically inferred and are not directly given. It is quite possible to accept the principle of causality while admitting with Hume that causal connections are not empirically intuited (or directly given). This does not necessarily mean that all causal connections are merely inferred (Chapter 9).

[10] A datum is theological in nature if the source of our knowledge of it goes back to some claimed divine revelation. That datum in turn can be known either by requiring faith as the exclusive source of its knowledge, or it can also be supported by natural reason. An example of the latter is the Mosaic teaching on murder as one of the Ten Commandments. This teaching goes back to (Judeo-Christian) divine revelation, but the evil of directly killing the innocent is obviously given via natural reason as well. In contrast, the Christian teaching on the doctrine of the Trinity cannot be established via natural reason alone, and therefore simply has to be accepted—if it is to be accepted at all—by religious faith alone. In this book, I will only make claims to theological truth from

examples that can also be verified by natural reason, which is in keeping with its theme of being a philosophy of psychology.

[11] For example, the whole realm of inner, psychological life is not directly accessible to empirical investigation.

[12] Edmund Husserl, *Logical Investigations*, 2nd ed., ed. Dermot Moran (London: Routledge, 2001), 168.

[13] For example, the *American Psychological Association* webpage states, "Using empirical methods, psychologists apply that universal curiosity to collect and interpret research data to better understand and solve some of society's most challenging problems." Science of Psychology, accessed on July 10, 2020, https://www.apa.org/action/science.

[14] This term literally means "to set limits to." At first it may appear as an overly restrictive or negative approach, but delimiting ideas are like rules to a game. Without them the game cannot exist. So, analogously, ideas that are not delimited become so vague and broad that they can mean everything, and therefore nothing. They become meaningless.

[15] Examples here will help. In psychology, Freud psychologizes religion in his book when he states that the idea of a personal God is nothing but a "wish-fulfillment as a prominent factor in its motivation and [a] disregard of its relations to reality."
Sigmund Freud, *The Future of an Illusion* (New York: Norton, 1989), 40.

Similarly, in philosophy Georg Hegel (1770-1831) thought that religion is merely symbolic and exists for simple, uneducated people who cannot understand philosophy, such as when he states, "In faith the true content is certainly already found, but there is still wanting to it the form of thought. All forms such as, we have already dealt with, feeling, popular ideas, and such like, may certainly have the form of truth, but they themselves are not the true form which makes the true content necessary. Thought is the absolute judge before which the content must verify and attest its claims."
Georg Hegel, *Lectures on the Philosophy of Religion*, Part III, trans. by Rev. E. B. Speirs & J. Burdon Sanderson (New York: Humanities Press, 1968), 148.

[16] The presence of thinking may be picked up by brain scans, but not the actual content of what someone else is thinking. Even if this content could be known, it would not be known "from the inside," as that other person knows it.

[17] For example, an eye cannot see itself. It can only see objects at a certain distance from itself, as over against itself.

[18] Plato, *Symposium*, in *The Dialogues of Plato*, trans. by B. Jowett (New York, Random House, 1937), 209e-212c.

[19] A common sense person is not here meant in any technical, philosophical sense. It simply means one who has a sense for what is clearly given as real and true. This kind of person may or may not be an intellectual or even particularly intelligent. They may or may not be able to articulate what he or she thinks.

[20] For example, the reason why contradictory assertions cannot both be true is because any given being cannot both have and not have a given predicate at the same time and in the same respect. Thus, the logical principle of non-contradiction (concerning assertions) is grounded in the metaphysical principle of non-contradiction (concerning real beings). If a real being could both exist and not exist simultaneously, contradictory assertions about them could then both be true.

[21] For a sustained analysis of philosophical methodology as applied to psychology, see James A. Harold, *Rationality Within Modern Psychological Theory: Integrating Philosophy and Empirical Science* (Lanham: Lexington, 2016).

[22] There is not a perfect symmetry between the opinions of the common sense person and intellectual intuition, insofar as the common sense person stays on the level of especially clear and "obvious" truths, whereas there are other things—both in philosophy and in mathematics—which only become self-evident on the basis of sustained thought.

[23] Logotherapy refers to a counseling approach developed by Victor Frankl (1905-1997) that especially focused on helping clients discover themselves by discovering meaning.

[24] Naturally, when students take "lab classes" and have a chance to perform some of these experiments, the role of "taking things on faith" is reduced. They will now be able to concretely see and prove certain things for themselves.

[25] By checking introductory psychology textbooks, one can verify the claim that the empirical method is literally one starting point. It is at the beginning of every single text I checked. These texts are: Spencer A. Rathus, *Psychology: Principles in Practice,* 2nd ed. (New York: Holt, 1984); Dennis Goon, *Introduction to Psychology: Gateways to Mind and Behavior* (United States: Wadsworth, 2001); Don Hockenbury and Sandra Hockenbury, *Psychology,* 4th ed. (New York: Worth Publishers, 2006); David G Myers., *Psychology,* 8th ed. (New York: Worth, 2007); Rod Plotnhik, *Introduction to Psychology,* 6th ed. (United States: Wadsworth, 2002); and John W. Santrock, *Psychology Essentials,* 2nd ed. (Boston: McGraw Hill, 2003).

[26] Later in the text (Chapter 7) I will call these powers *ontological powers* going back to our collective *first nature,* insofar as these powers are simply givens of our basic nature. What we do with these powers, the actual exercise of these powers, will refer to our *second nature.*

[27] Occasionally one hears how replicating experiments have become less important in modern science. This idea becomes less tempting after reading the following article by Ed Yong, "Psychology's Replication Crisis Is Running Out of Excuses." *The Atlantic,* accessed on Nov 19, 2018, https://www.theatlantic.com/science/archieve/2018/11/psychologys-replication-crisis-real/576223/.

[28] B. F. Skinner, *Beyond Freedom and Dignity* (Toronto: Bantam, 1972), 13.

[29] Later (Chapter 8) I will give a justification for this law of motivation by referring to Freud's discovery of the phenomenon of repression. It is only on the basis of this law of motivation that Freud's assertion of the phenomenon of repression makes sense.

[30] Thus, a person does not become intrinsically important when "valued" by another. Rather, every person is important in him or herself, independent of any act of "valuing."

There is, however, one sense in which values can be psychological. Think, for example, of an act of self-sacrificing love. This act is surely something important in itself, and it is a psychic act performed and brought into being by a person. So, even though *values* are fully objective properties of the being (including acts) that bear them—in that sense not produced by the person—the free *act* (of self-sacrificing love) which bears an intrinsic value is willed into being. In that sense some values are a psychological product of the person.

[31] Both *intrinsic value* and *subjectively satisfying* kinds of importance are technical philosophical terms going back to the philosophy of Dietrich von Hildebrand (1889-1977). See, *Ethics* (Chicago: Franciscan Herald Press, 1953), 34-63.

[32] For example, a person who is partially color blind will see colors differently than another person who is not.

[33] George Berkeley, *A Treatise Concerning the Principles of Human Knowledge* (Indianapolis: Bobbs-Merrill, 1957), 6.

34 An "ought" is not necessarily moral in nature. For example, I ought to appreciate something that is really beautiful, but that is hardly a moral ought. In contrast, I "ought"—in the moral sense—respect someone else's life and property.

35 The importance of pleasure *and displeasure* refers to the positive and negative manifestations of the same kind of importance that is dependent upon our subjectivity. For simplicity's sake, I will just speak of pleasure.

36 By "instinct" I mean a consciously experienced biological urge. Examples are a motherly instinct, instinct of self-preservation, sex instincts, and so forth.

37 Max Scheler, *Ressentiment*, trans. by Peter Heath (New York: Schoken Books, 1961), 45-6.

38 Ibid, 23.

39 Introjection is different from empathy. An empathetic person will "climb into the shoes" of another and try to feel what he or she is subjectively experiencing, but there is no confusing that other person's feelings with their own. With introjection, there is that confusion. There is something infantile, or at least childish, about introjection.

40 It is easy to notice small children merely repeating the opinions of their parents and thereby confusing their parents' opinions with their own. That seems to be a typical and normal stage of childhood development. To remain in such a state as an adult, however, is to be fixated at this immature stage of development.

41 Carl Rogers, "A Therapist's View of Personal Goals," Pendle Hill Pamphlet #108, (Wallingford, PA: Pendle Hill, 1959), 11.

42 An *immanent* state refers to the absence of *transcendence*. A transcendent relation is one that goes "beyond the self." For example, it is impossible to understand some response of love without bringing in the object of one's love, the beloved. In contrast, there are other psychic experiences which do not go beyond the self. They are instead merely explained in terms of one's own subjective needs or instincts, such as when a person simply lives for him or her self.

43 *American Psychological Association*, "Ethical Principles of Psychologists and Code of Conduct," Principle E: Respect for People's Rights and Dignity, accessed July 15, 2020, http://apa.org/ethics/code.

44 As is well known, Skinner goes beyond classical (Pavlovian) conditioning to what he terms "operant conditioning." Briefly, classical conditioning investigates controlling involuntary, automatic behaviors, while operant conditioning focuses on manipulating voluntary behavior via rewards or punishments. As will be discussed later (Chapter 7), voluntariness does not yet specifically imply personal freedom, insofar as animal behavior can be voluntary, but not free.
See, B. F Skinner, *Science and Human Behavior* (New York: Macmillan, 1953), 59-90.

45 Ibid, 139-40.

46 *Transcendence* refers to a going beyond the inner, subjective life of a person—oriented around a subjectivistic world of only appearances and illusions—to a knowledge of and a response to what is genuinely real and intrinsically good.

47 Later, at the end of Chapter 5, I will explain the reason why, concerning mathematical and philosophical objects, an intuition into some universal essences is possible. But empirical intuition, in contrast, only references (at least directly) individual instances and not its universal essence. Why? It is because of a different kind of intelligibility at stake. Mathematical/philosophical objects have a far higher kind of intelligibility than empirical objects.

[48] Something analogous to this idea of an "inside" and "outside" can be found in other spheres. For example, it is one thing to see another marriage, family or culture "from without." It is quite another thing, however, to see them "from within," such as with the experience of persons who are actually "in" the marriage, family or culture. Similarly, applying the empirical method to all psychic realities having an "inside" is not fully satisfying because this method only sees "from without."

[49] Goon, Dennis, *Introduction to Psychology: Gateways to Mind and Behavior* (United States: Wadsworth, 2001), 4.

[50] This point—concerning the different level of reality of inner conscious experience—will need development (Chapter 4). Here I can add that this radical distinction between brain and conscious experience can still exist while admitting to all kinds of relations between them. For example, proper brain physiology and biochemistry are empirically necessary conditions for right thinking. That such relations exist is not sufficient evidence for asserting any kind of identity between brain and mind.

[51] Just as a physical atmosphere can be clear or polluted, so analogously can there be other kinds of atmospheres, such as moral, cultural and intellectual atmospheres. And these other kinds can also in their own way be clear or polluted.

[52] At most this is only a kind of pseudo-obviousness, going back not to some rational insight or proof, but rather merely to a cultural assumption everyone within that culture tends to make.

[53] There is a real difference between philosophical speculation and philosophical insight. A real philosophical insight, such as *responsibility presupposes freedom* is necessarily true and cannot be otherwise. But where there is no insight, philosophers can still speculate or theorize about things. It is this speculation which can be mistaken.

[54] Augustine states, "What then, is time? There can be no quick and easy answer, for it is no simple matter even to understand what it is, let alone find words to explain it. Yet, in our conversation, no word is more familiarly used or more easily recognized than 'time.'" *Confessions*, Book 11, section 14 (London, Penguin: 1988), 263-4.

[55] Karen Horney, *The Neurotic Personality of Our Time* (New York: Norton, 1964), 69.

[56] This use of the term goes back to the philosophy of phenomenology, specifically to Edmund Husserl. A good introduction to this notion is found in Robert Sokolowski, *Introduction to Phenomenology,* (Cambridge: Cambridge University Press, 2000), 8-16.

This term (*intentionality*) has become especially important in the twentieth century philosophy of phenomenology. It can be traced back to medieval philosophy, but over time dropped out of philosophical discourse. The philosopher who re-introduced intentionality into modern philosophy was Franz Brentano (1838-1917), and the philosopher who especially developed this notion is the father of phenomenology, Edmund Husserl (1859-1938). Brentano thought intentionality characterized all of consciousness, that is, he thought that all conscious life is essentially or necessarily characterized as being "about something." Later philosophers will notice that there are some aspects of our conscious life which are non-intentional, such as what will be developed below in the text, concerning lateral self-presence.

[57] David Hume, *A Treatise of Human Nature,* ed. by L.A. Selby-Bigge (New York: Oxford University Press, 1951), 252.

[58] See B. F. Skinner, *Beyond Freedom and Dignity* (New York: Bantam, 1972), 21.

[59] Sigmund Freud, *The Ego and the Id,* trans. by Joan Riviere (New York: Norton, 1960), 4.

[60] David G. Myers, *Psychology,* 8th ed. (New York: Worth, 2007), 53.

[61] You cannot give what you do not have. Again, self-presence is synonymous with self-possession.

[62] The self which is only given laterally is not even known, because knowledge is essentially intentional (about something). Thus, the self needs to be further objectivized (or intentionalized) in order to be known. Self-presence is in contrast non-intentional in nature. It is associated with knowledge, an essential ingredient of knowledge, but something more is needed: some object known.

[63] Sir Isaac Newton, *Newton's Principia*, vol. 2, *The System of the World*, trans. by Andrew Motte, Rev. Florian Cajori (Berkeley: University of California Press, 1962), 547.

[64] William F. Lawhead, *A History of Western Philosophy* (Belmont: Wadsworth, 1995), 290.

[65] Here is Augustine's argument in his own words, "So when it is bidden to know itself, it should not start looking for itself as though it had drawn off from itself, but should draw off what it has added to itself. *For it is more inward, not only than these sensible things which are obviously outside*, but also than their images which are in a part of the soul that animals have too, though they lack intelligence which is proper to the mind" [Italics added].
De Trinitate, trans. by Edmund Hill (Brooklyn: New City Press, 1996), Book X, 295.

[66] Actually, a person who is nothing but a "mere slave"—in some metaphysical/ontological sense—does not exist. It is at most an external state going against the human being's nature that is then illegitimately applied to some human persons.

[67] Aristotle asserts, "For it is at the beginning that the mistake is committed in these cases, and as the beginning according to the proverb is half the whole, i.e., is as important as all the rest, it follows that even a small mistake at the beginning of any affair bears the same proportion, i.e., is equivalent to the mistakes at all the other points." *Politics of Aristotle*, in *Introduction to Aristotle*, trans. by Richard McKeon, (Chicago: University of Chicago Press, 1973), 1301b, 351.

[68] In this text I will use the terms *state of affairs* and *fact* synonymously.

[69] These psychic affective feelings are distinct from bodily feelings, such as the pain a person feels when, say, someone is hit by a fastball pitch. Both are felt, but the first in "felt" in the soul and the second in the body. Although bodily pains are felt "in" the body, they are not felt "by" the body, but by the soul. For example, people will often report their arm hurting after it has been amputated.

[70] In contrast, to be affectively attracted to that which is evil, disordered or dishonorable is not a gift at all, but a curse.

[71] This expression, "ontological inauthenticity," is meant to suggest a basic contradiction between the way persons live their life with the kind of being they in fact possess.

[72] There are products of intellectual acts that are clearly psychologically inspired. Here I am thinking of things like idol worship in religion, and virtue signaling, value blindness, scapegoating in ethics, obsessions and compulsions in psychology, all of which seem to have a strong psychological component for understanding them. Specifically, one can ask about them: what is the psychological benefit that accrues for indulging these things? I will not discuss these topics here, as they will be covered over the course of this text.

[73] Carl Rogers, *On Becoming a Person* (Boston: Houghton, 1961), 185-6.

[74] Later in this Chapter I will claim that there are also certain psychic acts and responses that can "live through time," such as with the lover towards his beloved. The real lover does not merely love the beloved when he is thinking explicitly of her, but also this love "colors" his conscious life even when he is not thinking of her.

75 Rogers, *On Becoming*, 189.

76 Carl Rogers, *Becoming Partners: Marriage and Its Alternatives* (New York: Dell, 1970), 10; quoted by Paul Vitz, *Psychology as Religion: The Cult of Self-Worship* (Grand Rapids: Eerrdmans, 1994), 59.

77 If *being is perceiving*, then the mountain is nothing but its sensible appearance. This is an instance of an empiric*ism* which denies the substantial reality of the mountain because the notion of substance, like that of value, are both non-empirical predicates of a being.

78 Here I am referring to an appearance *as an appearance*, such as the qualities of big or small, and not the being which appears, such as a mountain. Surely a mountain makes a claim to objectivity, but its bigness or smallness does not. Even Mt. Everest appears big as seen from land, but small from the moon.

79 From an ultimate metaphysical point of view, there is a dimension of goodness to everything that is, including dust on a desk. However, from the point of view of our motivation, many things strike us as being neutral in importance.

80 Although this section includes moral character formation, I do not wish to imply that depression and despair are always moral vices. These particular miseries can, but do not necessarily have a moral quality.

81 Soren Kierkegaard, *Sickness Unto Death*, in *Fear and Trembling and The Sickness Unto Death*, trans. by Walter Lowrie (Princeton: Princeton University Press, 1968), 157.

82 C. S. Lewis, *The Abolition of Man* (New York: Macmillan, 1955), 32-33.

83 The human soul then is substantially distinct from the body, but is also incomplete, needing the body to form the full human being. A soul without its body is an incomplete substance.

84 The work of Gregor Mendel (1822-1884), the father of genetics, comes to mind here as one among many other examples of someone not interested nor even aware of the practical application of his scientific work.

85 John Watson, *Behaviorism* (New York: Norton, 1958), 5.

86 Ibid, 4.

87 David G. Myers, *Psychology*, 8th ed. (New York: Worth, 2007), 571-72.

88 It is worthwhile noting just how disrespectful this approach is to other persons: manipulating them instead of appealing directly to their intellect so that they could see the truth of some proposition for themselves. The opposite attitude to Skinner is the respectful approach (to other persons) of Socrates.

89 Myers, *Psychology*, 53.

90 The distinction between non-conscious and un-conscious states goes back to a distinction between two kinds of opposition: contradictory and contrary opposition. A contradictory opposition refers to a simple absence of something, such as the contradictory opposite of "X" (whatever X is) is the simple absence of it (non-X). So, if a being—like a rock—is itself unrelated to consciousness, it is non-conscious. A contrary opposite refers to more than just a simple absence, insofar as it implies a kind of attack upon some being (whatever X is). Thus, for example, a contrary opposite of justice is not merely the simple absence of it (the absence of justice, say, in a dog), it is rather some manifest injustice (an attack upon what is just), such as my taking something that does not belong to me. Thus, a being that is merely non-conscious only refers to a simple absence, like a rock. But a being that is unconscious is one that is ordered to consciousness, but for whatever reason, cannot actualize it.

91 Closely related to the topic of learning theory is developmental psychology. As important as this topic is for psychology, I will not discuss it here.

92 See Dietrich von Hildebrand, *What is Philosophy?* (New York: Routledge, 1990), chap. 4.

93 Paul C. Vitz, "The Origin of Consciousness in the Integration of Analog (Right Hemisphere) & Digital (Left Hemisphere) Codes," *Journal of Consciousness Exploration & Research*, Vol. 8, Issue 11, 881-906.

94 Ibid, 883.

95 Explaining animal learning by the application of mere instinct or by conditioning does not do justice to this kind of rationality.

96 C. S. Lewis, *Mere Christianity* (New York: Macmillan, 1952), 32.

97 Edward Dougherty, "Science without Validation in a World without Meaning," *American Affairs*, accessed on July 16, 2020, https://americanaffairsjournal.org/2020/05/science-without-validation-in-a-world-without-meaning/.

98 The reason why no intuition is given with respect to *zebraness* can be explained by the box entitled, "Intelligibility" (see Chapter 5). Philosophical essences possess the highest kind of intelligibility such that no inductive generalizations are necessary: a person can directly grasp the universal essence structure of, say, responsibility to "see" with strict necessity that it presupposes freedom. But, in contrast, with *zebraness*, one cannot discover a strictly necessary reason for why zebras need to be striped. It seems to be a relatively "brute" fact that zebras are striped (while granting the stripes make zebras more difficult to see by predators from distances).

99 There is also inference to best explanation. See below in this chapter.

100 I grant that some objects of consciousness are material in nature and thereby sensibly perceived. It remains true that consciousness itself is neither material nor sensibly perceived.

101 Earlier (Chapter 5) I gave an example of this with the psychology of John Watson, who absurdly denied the existence of inner psychic states (specifically, the conscious act of denying) while—in the very same sentence—presupposed their existence.

102 See Samir Okasha, *Philosophy of Science: A Very Short Introduction* (Oxford: Oxford University Press, 2002), 29-33.

103 Gilbert Ryle characterizes Descartes' body/soul relation in this way, "The Newtonian system is no longer the sole paradigm of natural science. Man need not be degraded to a machine by being denied to be *a ghost in a machine*. He might, after all, be a sort of animal, namely, a higher mammal. There has yet to be ventured the hazardous leap to the hypothesis that perhaps he is a man" (italics added). Gilbert Ryle, *The Concept of Mind* (Chicago: University of Chicago Press, 1949), 328.

104 It is interesting how psychology is turning to a narrative approach to personality theory and counseling. Thus, Paul Vitz states, "For example, recent theorists such as Roy Shafter, Donald Spence, Jerome Bruner, and Dan McAdams have emphasized a narrative understanding of personality, as well as storytelling aspects of knowledge in general and of the therapeutic session in particular." Paul Vitz, "Psychology in Recovery," *First Things*, No. 151 (March 2005): 18.

105 Thanks here to Prof. John Crosby.

106 Theological claims come in two basic varieties: those that can be verified by natural reason and those going beyond natural reason requiring religious faith. Since this work focuses on philosophy that works by way of natural reason, whatever theological claims

I make in this text will go back to this first type and thus can stand on their own independent of some specific religious authority..

[107] Paul Vitz, "Addressing Moderate Interpersonal Hatred Before Addressing Forgiveness in Psychotherapy and Counseling: A Proposed Model," *Journal of Religion and Health*, April 2018, vol. 57, Number 2, 730.

[108] Paul Vitz, *Psychology as Religion: The Cult of Self-Worship* (Grand Rapids: Eerdmans, 1994), 99.

[109] Ibid., 100. The passages quoted by Vitz are from Harry Emerson Fosdick, *As I See Religion* (New York: Harper, 1932), chap. 2.

[110] Matthew, 6, 1-4.

[111] Matthew, 7 4-5.

[112] In fact, rational psychology theoretically "stands on its own" in a far better way than empirical psychology, insofar as the latter presupposes (implicitly or explicitly) non-empirical psychic experiences (Chapter 6) outside its own methodology. Rational psychology, in contrast, presupposes nothing exterior to its own frame of reference.

[113] B.F Skinner, *Science and Human Behavior* (New York: Macmillan, 1953), 13.

[114] Pure chaos would also spell the death knell for our rational nature, insofar as the objective condition for the application of that nature, which is intelligibility, would be missing.

[115] Rationality, at least in a fully personal sense, refers to knowing and responding to things as they are in themselves and in the intellectual "light" of universal essences. Animals are not rational in that sense. Later in this chapter the case will be made for animals possessing a lower kind of rationality, not reducible to sense perception or instincts, on the one hand; nor do they possess this distinctly personal kind of rationality, on the other. Animals seem to understand individual things only in their individual, concrete nature, which allows them to solve simple puzzles. They cannot, however, see these individual things in the light of their universal essence.

[116] Charles Taylor, "Buffered and Porous Selves," *The Immanent Frame: Secularism, Religion and the Public Square*, September 2, 2008, accessed on July 16, 2020, https://tif.ssrc.org/2008/09/02buffered-and-porous-selves/.

[117] Putting the prefix, "non-" refers to the simple absence of something. It is the contradictory opposite of the following term. Thus, "being" and "non-being" are *contradictory* opposites. The relation between "rational" and "irrational," in contrast, is a *contrary* opposite. Its sense is to imply "an attack upon" something else, such as an attack upon rationality. A non-rational being implies no attack upon rationality. A contrary opposite is a more radical kind of opposition than a contradictory opposite.

[118] Consider Sartre's own words,

> What is meant here by saying that existence precedes essence? It means that, first of all, man exists, turns up, appears on the scene, and, only afterwards, defines himself. If man, as the existentialist conceived him, is indefinable, it is because at first he is nothing. Only afterward will he be something, and he himself will have made what he will be. Thus, there is no human nature, since there is no God to conceived it. Not only is man what he conceives himself to be, but he is also only what he wills himself to be after this thrust toward existence.

Sartre, Jean-Paul, "The Humanism of Existentialism," in *Existentialism: Basic Writings*, Charles Guignon and Derk Pereboom, eds. (Indianapolis: Hackett, 2001), 292-3.

Excerpted from Sartre, Jean-Paul, *Existentialism and Human Emotion* (New York: Citadel Press, 1957).

119 This lack of self-possession explains why it is that it is no violation of an animal's nature for a person to own it. In fact, it is often just the opposite, where dogs (for instance) are especially fulfilled in being owned by loving masters.

120 *Aristotle's Politics*, in *Introduction to Aristotle*, trans. by Richard McKeon, Book 1, 1253A (Chicago: U. of Chicago Press, 1973), 599.

121 Analogous relations refer to a real similarity, but within the context of an utter difference of kind. For example, consider the notion of *power* from the following two points of view: water and mind power. There is an obvious real similarity here, justifying the use of the same word, power. But this similarity does not hide the radical difference between them, such that there is a difference of kind and not merely that of degree. For example, merely adding more water (quantitatively) one can never "reach" anything like mind power, because the difference is one of kind (qualitative), not of degree.

122 Obviously, when an animal pet becomes part of a human family, it will often defend the family. Its "species" in this context will then be larger than its own biological species to include its adoptive family.

123 It is worthwhile giving the full quote.

> I forgot that every little action of the common day makes or unmakes character, and that therefore what one has done in the recent chamber one has some day to cry aloud on the housetop. I ceased to be Lord over myself. I was no longer captain of my own soul, and did not know it. I allowed pleasure to dominate me. I ended in horrible disgrace. There is only one thing for me now, absolute humility.

Oscar Wilde, *De Profundis*, in the *Collected Works of Oscar Wilde: the Plays, the Poems the Stories and the Essays, Including De Profundis* (Hertfordshire: Wordsworth, 2007), 1071.

124 Daniel Robinson, *An Intellectual History of Psychology* (Madison: University of Wisconsin Press, 1995), 102.

125 Josef Pieper, *Leisure the Basis of Culture* (New York: Pantheon, 1952), 107.

126 I know I was. I remember precisely the very first time in my life having this thought. I was a high school sophomore in a class discussing Aldous Huxley's, *Brave New World*. I thought, what was so wrong with people being kept (politically and socially) "in their place" if they are continuously enticed by pleasure after pleasure? Seemed like a good deal to me. What is so bad about that?

127 Robert Roberts, *Spiritual Emotions: A Psychology of Christian Virtues* (Grand Rapids: Eerdmans, 2007), 56.

128 Scott Peck, *People of the Lie* (New York: Touchstone, 1983), 77.

129 Sigmund Freud, "The Loss of Reality in Neurosis and Psychosis," in *General Psychological Theory: Papers on Metapsychology*, trans. by Philip Rieff (New York, Macmillan, 1963), 204.

130 Dietrich and Alice von Hildebrand, *The Art of Living* (Chicago: Franciscan Herald Press, 1965), 33-4.

131 *Man's Search for Meaning*, trans. by Ilsa Lasch, (Boston: Beacon Press, 2006), 84. See also Friedrich Nietzsche, who states, "If you have your *why?* for life, then you can get along with almost any *how?*" In *Twilight of the Idols*, "Maxims and Arrows," §12, trans. by Duncan Large (New York: OUP Oxford, 1998), 7.

[132] For example, let us assume that Carl Jung is right and there exists an archaic idea (archetype) within our collective unconscious of the notion of the Wise Old Man. Investigation of the evidence for such an idea need not take into account the living, true, transcendent God. This would be a purely (immanent) psychological investigation.

[133] Michelle A. Cretella, "Gender Dsyphoria in Children and Suppression of Debate," *Journal of American Physicians and Surgeons 21* (Summer 2016): 51.

[134] Ryan Anderson gives various anecdotal stories of people who actually went through sex change operations, who then came to regret the procedure because their underlying psychological problems did not evaporate with the transition. See, *When Harry Became Sally: Responding to the Transgender Moment* (New York: Encounter, 2018), 17.

[135] Here I am thinking of something like tolerance or tradition. See Dietrich von Hildebrand, *Graven Images: Substitutes for True Morality* (Steubenville: Hildebrand Press, 2019), Chapter 3.

[136] *Mere Christianity* (New York: Macmillan, 1952), 22-23.

[137] See Dietrich von Hildebrand, *Ethics* (Chicago: Franciscan Herald Press, 1953), 299-309. I switch the order of his presentation of these two perfections only for my own convenience.

[138] Sam Harris, "Sam Harris on the Illusion of Free Will," *You Tube* video, accessed on Jan 28, 2018, https://youtu.be/7t_Uyi9bNS4accessed on Jan 28, 2017.

[139] The distinction between "causes and conditions" and rational reasons is very old in philosophy. See Plato, *Phaedo,* trans. by David Gallop (Oxford: Oxford, 1993) 54-55 (98c-99d).

[140] "Bipolar" is here only meant in a geometrical sense—as a single reality presupposing two dimensions or "poles"—than in any psychiatric sense.

[141] Robert Bolt, *A Man for all Seasons* (London: Samuel French, 1962), 98. I am grateful to Dr. John Crosby for this example.

[142] Sam Harris, "Sam Harris on the Illusion of Free Will," *You Tube* video. For an interesting and accessible discussion distinguishing chance (or luck) with design, see William A. Dembski, "The Third Mode of Explanation: Detecting Evidence of Intelligent Design in the Universe," in *Science and Evidence for Design in the Universe* (San Francisco: Ignatius, 2000), 20-31.

[143] Alan Wheelis, "Will and Psychoanalysis," *Journal of the American Psychoanalytic Association,* IV/2 April, 1956, 256.

[144] Psychoanalytic therapists generally follow the lead of the originator of their school, Sigmund Freud, who is a famous determinist. For example, he states, "The truth is that you have an illusion of a psychic freedom within you which you do not want to give up. I regret to say that on this point I find myself in sharpest opposition to your views." Sigmund Freud, *A General Introduction to Psychoanalysis,* trans. by Joan Riviere (Garden City: Garden City Books, 1952), 45.

Bibliography

American Psychological Association. "Ethical Principles of Psychologists and Code of Conduct." Principle E: Respect for People's Rights and Dignity. Accessed July 15, 2020. http://apa.org.

Anderson, Ryan. *When Harry Became Sally: Responding to the Transgender Moment.* New York: Encounter, 2018.

Aristotle. *Politics.* In *Introduction to Aristotle.* Translated by Richard McKeon. Chicago: University of Chicago Press.

Augustine. *The Confessions of St. Augustine.* Translated by John K. Ryan. New York: Image Book, 1960.

_____. *De Trinitate.* Translated by Edmund Hill. Brooklyn: New City Press, 1996.

Barron, Bishop Robert. "Bishop Robert Barron sets sights on America's secular culture." *Aleteia.* Accessed July 1, 2021. https://aleteia.org/2018/06/11/bishop-robert-barron-sets-sights-on-americas-secular-culture/.

Berkeley, George. *A Treatise Concerning the Principles of Human Knowledge.* Indianapolis: Bobbs-Merrill, 1967.

Bolt, Robert. *A Man for all Seasons.* London: Samuel French, 1962.

Cretella, Michelle A. "Gender Dysphoria in Children and Suppression of Debate." *Journal of American Physicians and Surgeons.* Volume 21, Number 2. Summer 2016.

Dembski, William A. "The Third Mode of Explanation: Detecting Evidence of Intelligent Design in the Sciences." *Science and Evidence for Design in the Universe.* San Francisco: Ignatius, 2000.

Dougherty, Edward. "Science without Validation in a World without Meaning," *American Affairs.* Accessed on July 16, 2020, https://americanaffairsjournal.org/2020/05/science-without-validation-in-a-world-without-meaning/.

Fosdick, Harry Emerson. *As I See Religion.* New York: Harper, 1932.

Frankl, Victor. *Man's Search for Meaning.* Translated by Ilsa Lasch. Boston: Beacon Press, 2006.

Freud, Sigmund. *The Ego and the Id.* Translated by Joan Riviere. New York: Norton, 1960.

_____. *The Future of an Illusion.* Translated by W. D. Robson Scott. New York: Norton, 1989.

_____. *A General Introduction to Psychoanalysis.* Translated by Joan Riviere. New York: Garden City Books, 1952.

_____. *General Psychological Theory: Papers on Metapsychology.* Translated by Philip Rieff. New York: Macmillan, 1963.

Goon, Dennis. *Introduction to Psychology: Gateways to Mind and Behavior.* United States: Wadsworth, 2001.

Harold, James. *Rationality Within Modern Psychological Theory: Integrating Philosophy and Empirical Science.* Lanham: Lexington, 2016.

Harris, Sam. "Sam Harris on the Illusion of Free Will." *YouTube* video. Accessed on Jan 28, 2017, https://youtu.be/7t_Uyi9bNS4.

Hegel, Georg. *Lectures on the Philosophy of Religion*. Translated by Rev. E. B. Speirs. New York: Humanities Press, 1968.

Hildebrand, Dietrich von. *Ethics*. Chicago: Franciscan Herald Press, 1953.

_____. *What is Philosophy?* New York: Routledge, 1990.

Hildebrand, Dietrich von, and Alice Jourdain. *The Art of Living*. Chicago: Franciscan Herald Press, 1965.

_____. *Graven Images: The Substitutes for a True Morality*. New York: McKay, 1957.

Hockenbury, Don and Sandra Hockenbury. *Psychology*. Fourth Edition. New York: Worth Publishers, 2006.

Horney, Karen. *The Neurotic Personality of Our Time*. New York: Norton, 1964.

Hume, David. *A Treatise of Human Nature*. Edited by L. A. Selby-Bigge. New York: Oxford University Press, 1951.

Husserl, Edmund. *Logical Investigations*. Translated by Dermot Moran. Second Edition. London: Routledge, 2001.

James, William. *Pragmatism*. New York: Macmillan, 1960.

Kierkegaard, Soren. *Sickness Unto Death*. Translated by Walter Lowrie. Princeton: Princeton University Press, 1968.

Lawhead, William F. *A History of Western Philosophy*. Belmont: Wadsworth, 1995.

Lewis, C. S. *The Abolition of* Man. New York: Macmillan, 1955.

_____. *Mere Christianity*. New York: Macmillan, 1952.

Myers, David G. *Psychology*. Eighth Edition. New York: Worth, 2007.

Newton, Sir Isaac. *Newton's Principia*, vol. 2, *The System of the World*. Translated by Andrew Motte and Rev. Florian Cajori. Berkeley: University of California Press, 1962.

Nietzsche, Friedrich. *Twilight of the Idols*. Translated by Ilsa Lasch. Boston: Beacon Press, 2006.

Okasha, Samir. *Philosophy of Science: A Very Short Introduction*. Oxford: Oxford University Press, 2002.

Pieper, Josef. *Leisure: The Basis of Culture*. Translated by Alexander Dru. New York: Pantheon, 1952.

Plato. *Symposium*. Translated by Benjamin Jowett. New York: Washington Square Press, 1950.

_____. *Phaedo*. Translated by David Gallop. Oxford: Oxford, 1993.

Peck, Scott. *People of the Lie*. New York: Touchstone, 1983.

Plotnik, Rod. *Introduction to Psychology*. Sixth Edition. United States: Wadsworth, 2002.

Rathus, Spencer A. *Psychology: Principles in Practice*. Second Edition. New York: Holt, 1984.

Roberts, Robert. *Spiritual Emotions: A Psychology of Christian Virtues*. Grand Rapids: Eerdmans, 2007.

Robinson, Daniel. *An Intellectual History of Psychology*. Madison: University of Wisconsin Press, 1995.

Rogers, Carl. *On Becoming a Person.* Boston: Houghton, 1961.

_____. *Becoming Partners: Marriage and Its Alternatives.* New York: Dell, 1970.

_____. "A Therapist's View of Personal Goals." Pendle Hill Pamphlet. Wallingford: Pendle Hill #108, 1959.

Ryle, Gilbert. *The Concept of Mind.* Chicago: University of Chicago Press, 1949.

Santrock, John. *Psychology Essentials.* Second Edition. Boston: McGraw Hill, 2003.

Sartre, Jean-Paul. *Existentialism and Human Emotion.* Translated by Bernard Frechtman. New York: Citadel Press, 1957.

Scheler, Max. *Ressentiment.* Translated by Peter Heath. New York: Schocken Books, 1961.

Skinner, B. F. *Beyond Freedom and Dignity.* Toronto: Bantam, 1972.

_____. *Science and Human Behavior.* New York: Macmillan, 1953.

_____. *Upon Further Reflection.* New York: Dover, 1986.

Sokolowski, Robert. *Introduction to Phenomenology.* Cambridge: Cambridge University Press, 2000.

Taylor, Charles. "Buffered and Porous Selves." The Immanent Frame: Secularism Religion, and the Public Square. Accessed on July 16, 2020. https://tif.ssrc.org/2008/09/02buffered-and-porous-selves/.

Vitz, Paul. "Addressing Moderate Interpersonal Hatred Before Addressing Forgiveness in Psychotherapy and Counseling: A Proposed Model." *Journal of Religion and Health.* April 2018, Volume 57, Number 2.

_____. "The Origin of Consciousness in the Integration of Analog (Right Hemisphere) & Digital (Left Hemisphere) Codes." *Journal of Consciousness & Research.* December 2017, Volume 8, Issue 11, 881-906.

_____. "Psychology in Recovery." *First Things.* New York: Institute for Religion and Public Life, March 2005.

_____. *Psychology as Religion: The Cult of Self-Worship.* Grand Rapids: Eerdmans, 1994.

Vitz, Paul C., William J. Nordling, and Craig Steven Titus, editors, *A Catholic Meta-Model of the Person: Integration with Psychology & Mental Health Practice.* Sterling VA: Divine Mercy University Press, 2020.

Watson, John. *Behaviorism.* New York: Norton, 1958.

Wheelis, Alan. "Will and Psychoanalysis." *Journal of the American Psychoanalytic Association.* IV/2 April 1956.

Wilde, Oscar. *De Profundis.* In *The Collected Works of Oscar Wilde: The Plays, the Poems, the Stories and the Essays, Including De Profundis.* Hertfordshire: Wordsworth, 2007.

Yong, Ed. "Psychology's Replication Crisis Is Running Out of Excuses." *The Atlantic.* Accessed March 2020. https://www.theatlantic.com/science/archive/2018/11/psychologys-replication-crisis-real/576223/?utm_term=2018-11-19T20%3A27%3A34&utm_camp aign=the-atlantic&utm_source=facebook&utm_content=edit-promo&utm_medium=social&fbclid=IwAR1FMKYGEo-TyO9_sIi6-s3_0m1ro7Vf 5sXXmqsx_frgz6IHeyaxzL_JqPE.

Index

A

analysis, 11–13, *See also* synthesis
anger, 76–77
animal voluntariness, 116
anorexia nervosa, 127
appearance, 26–28, 33–34
    subjectivity of, 62–63
Aquinas, Thomas, xii, 130
Aristotle, 50, 63, 73, 115
    distinguishing incontinence
        from intemperance, 38–39
Augustine, xii, 47, 58
Austen, Jane, 105
authenticity, 33

B

behavior, 80–86
    and inner conscious life, 41–42
    two senses of, 80
Berkeley, George, 70
body dysmorphic disorder (BDD),
    127
body integrity identity disorder
    (BIID), 127
Bolt, Robert, 138
brain, 55–59
Brentano, Franz, 154

C

cause, 59, 86
    distinguished from a condition,
        86–88
    first (uncaused) and second
        (caused) causes, 87

character, 134–35
common sense, 14–17
consciousness
    distinguishing unconscious
        from non-consciousn states,
        88
    privacy of, 22–23
countertransference, 17
Cretella, Michelle, 127
cultural prisms, 45

D

de Wulf, Maurice, 119
Descartes, Rene, 103
descriptive meaning, 128–29, *See
    also* prescriptive meaning
despair, 76–77
Dostoyevsky, Fyodor, 105
dualism, two forms of, 103–4

E

empiric*ism*, 5, 8, 43, 45, 145
    psychological, 21
envy, 32
experience, lived, 10–11
    psychological, 13–15
expression, bodily, 103

F

first and second nature, 114, 115,
    128
    and self-determination, 114
first principle of psychology, 63–64
Fosdick, Harry Emerson, 108